Hair
In Search of Natural Beauty

Kaname MORITA

SAIRYUSHA Co., Ltd.

Hair

In Search of Natural Beauty

Published by SAIRYUSHA Co., Ltd.
DAIKO bld. 6F
3-10, Kanda-Jimbocho, Chiyoda-ku,
Tokyo, 101-0051, JAPAN

https://www.sairyusha.co.jp/

ISBN978-4-7791-2881-3 C0077

This book is a translation of『髪　あるがままの美しさを求めて』
written by Kaname MORITA (Tsubanasha 2021).

Translation by
Chie Matsumoto
Sam Matsumoto-Ripp

A Passage to Hair Restoration

The vision for restoration

When you change the way you think,
your habits and future will change as well.

1. Remember the way hair salons used to be.
2. Cut your hair to get it in better shape.
3. Try to make your hair beautiful by yourself.
4. Get your hair in better shape by enjoying the smell and feel of plants and flowers.
5. Stop using chemicals (e.g. hair colors and perms, and etc).
6. Change your shampooing habits.

Hair restoration methods and the process

What's important here is to understand them and repeat them.

1. Get your hair into better shape by trimming it. (By doing so, you use less henna so you can cut costs.) This also promotes more durability. Design the cut only using newly grown hair.
2. Revive the hair by using henna. The strength of hair increases with its help. It also helps remove dirt from hair and scalp. Beautiful hair will grow due to the antioxidants in the henna.
3. Choose your shampoo. (Lakshmi sells shampoos with excellent biodegradation power.)

"Treatment during the transition from damaged hair to beautiful hair"

Use liquid shampoo or treatments with moisturizing effects.

“How to treat beautiful hair specifically, different from the repair process”

Use liquid shampoo less often. Do not use treatment. Wash your hair only with water and plants. (Lakshmi recommends the “Migushi-Sumashi” product line)

Time and money should be spent for restoring hair

“Beautiful hair” is a reflection of your inner beauty

1. Cost — You can keep the cost of your lifetime hair treatment down to less than a tenth of what they would be at a salon by giving yourself treatments.
2. Time — You can save much time by giving yourself a hair treatment at home (everything besides cutting your own hair).
3. Relaxation outside of hair salons — Relax yourself and improve your mental health by spending more time outside hair salons doing things such as reading and going to museums, concerts, movies, etc.

Completion of beautiful hair restoration

Once the chemically “damaged hair” is transformed into “beautiful hair” healed by plants, the only thing left to do is to care for your hair with the ideal plant-based products. All of this can be done at home.

1. Design your haircuts only with new hair. Durable hair is grown. This is equivalent to curing/aging wood for construction.
2. By taking care of your own hair, you will change the way you feel about your hair.
3. As you repeat these actions, you will make your hair even more beautiful. By making these processes a habit, you can change your future.

In writing this book, I would like to share the best method that I was able to develop after more than 40 years of experience in the field of beauty for as many people as possible who aim to have beautiful hair.

Kaname MORITA

*Lakshmi is a cosmetic company that Kaname Morita owns.

Preface

In 1978, after graduating from beauty school, I was employed at a beauty salon in Tokyo. I also worked at a beauty salon in Nagasaki Prefecture before eventually returning. Upon my return, I began to feel uncomfortable with the way I had been working as a hairstylist, and I considered becoming independent in order to pursue the work I wanted to do. In 1984, six years after I started working as a beautician, I decided to become fully independent and open my own store.

I had two potential options. One was to open a salon in Kamakura City, Kanagawa Prefecture. The store would be a branch of Le Claire, which was run by one of the "Four Kings" of the beauty industry, Mr. Chikashi Tanaka. I was introduced to him by the owner of the beauty salon I worked at in Nagasaki. Mr. Tanaka was the first Japanese to be in charge of hair-styling for the Vogue magazine, so the idea of being in charge of one of Mr. Tanaka's stores was very appealing to me.

The other choice that I had was to open my own store and become completely independent. A colleague helped me find a beauty salon for sale. I discovered upon acquiring the building that Shin Yoshino, the artistic director of Vidal Sassoon in New York, had owned the building previously under the name "Atelier Shin."

After much thought, I chose to take a bit of a leap and start from scratch. This choice was a major turning point in my life, partially because of three things left behind in Yoshino's salon.

The first was Yoshino's writing, a pamphlet that introduced his work, titled "A pitfall of common sense."

The second was the book, "The Poetry of Existence: Monk OSHO," written by Bhagwan Sri Rajneesh (translation by Swami Prem Prabuddha, Merukumar Publishing Co, 1977), and the third was a powder made of a plant known as henna.

"A pitfall of common sense"

"When we notice that we are questioning 'rules' or 'common sense,' we are discovering a hole in the presented logic. We should not dismiss these holes, for they could become serious problems later on." I realized after hearing these words that I must face my issues without fear because of the possible consequences of ignoring one.

When I first started working at a beauty salon after attending vocational school, they told us never to question our seniors. We were not supposed to ask questions. It was considered a good thing to concentrate on taking in daily teachings without questioning them and to train our skills as a beautician. Despite being told this, I always had doubts and wonders.

When dyeing gray hair, we were supposed to dye it all in the same color, evenly. It was considered a basic beauty standard. However, I felt that it looked artificial and unnatural for a woman in her late 80s to have every part of her hair dyed the same color. Why did we work by such a rule? I asked my seniors this question, but they ignored me.

One day, I was given the task of applying color to a client in her late 80s. I had to try my new idea. I tried to create a more natural look by dyeing her hair in a few bundles and applying the colorant. This was my effort to put an end to the unnaturalness of pitch-black hair, without asking permission. I felt that it would give the hair a more natural look and feel. Somehow, I knew it would look better, and I wanted to experiment with that.

When I finished dyeing her hair, my superior said, “What are you doing? You're going to have to do this one all over again. Do you know what you are using the colorant for? You’re supposed to be using it to make beautiful black hair.”

My superior reprimanded me in the backroom, but the client was very happy. The senior staff member saw her off, acting the whole time as though nothing had happened.

On her next visit, she asked me to use the same technique on her hair again. Through this experience, I learned that the job of a hair stylist is to help reveal the beauty that clients never realize they have.

I had some doubts while I was learning perming and coloring techniques and treating customers' hair. I wondered why the more we tried to make their hair appear beautiful the more it seemed to get damaged. We applied treatment to ease the damage. When the customer came back; however, their hair appeared to be even more damaged. Were we doing this right? I strongly felt that we needed to revise our techniques after observing this.

To prove my theory, I needed data. After a thorough study of my data, I would formulate a hypothesis, and conduct an experiment. I would then plan a method to solve various questions that came to my mind. To reach a conclusion, I created a map and set out on a journey, which brings me to where I am now.

I wanted to know the truth. As I sought solutions for questions I had, I became more convinced that we could not achieve healthy, beautiful hair with care being the way it was. I came to the conclusion that we need to change our policies surrounding hair care to make hair more beautiful.

We need an economic system in which we can maintain our own natural beauty without damaging our hair. We should have a system where everyone involved in hair care can live happily without damaging their beautiful hair and health, without suffering any negative effects from dyeing or coloring. We need an economic system that allows us to do this; a system where everyone can be positive. We need to rethink hair care as we know it today.

This second passage discusses another one of the three things that were left at Atelier Shin; "The Poetry of Existence: Monk OSHO," written by Bhagwan Sri Rajneesh.

Based on the Tibetan esoteric teachings of Mahamudra, the book discusses the ultimate experience of a modern Indian thinker known as Osho. Born in India, Bhagwan Shri Rajneesh gave talks throughout India after nine years of teaching philosophy at the University of Jabalpur. After reading this book, my interest in India grew. I began to feel a deep connection to India. I never expected this when I first came across this book.

The third and final object I had found at Atelier Shin was henna. Shin Yoshino was based in New York at the time and occasionally returned to Japan to take appointments at his salon in Minami Aoyama, Tokyo. The henna left at the salon was a product that was sold in New

York. This was my first experience with actual henna. I began researching it, and it has guided me to where I am today.

I feel that Atelier Shin was the start of my life as a hairdresser.

Hair (*Kami*) is God (*Kami*)
When I set myself before hair
This is what I value

Why do we call hair *kami* in Japanese? Hiroshi Aramata explains the reason in his book, "A Cultural History of Hair (Ushio Publishing Co)," as follows:

> "Generally speaking, the Japanese believed that there were gods in the heavens, so they used the word kami, which means above, to mean god. Naturally, they came to believe that the god, or the soul, residing in the human body also resides in the hair, which is located above the rest of the body. In the ancient Japanese language, however, the word was not pronounced the same as how it is pronounced today. It had many more sounds than modern Japanese. After the Heian Era (794-1185), pronunciation became less distinct so it makes sense that the three words of heavens, hair and god ended up sounding very similar."

He also points out that people in other parts of the world also think of hair as being related to the gods.

> "The sun provides great natural energy that nurtures life on

> Earth. This energy is transmitted to Earth by its rays. People in the ancient times thought of these rays as the 'hair of the sun.' Thus, they imagined the sun as 'a god with long, shiny hair and a long beard.' The sun gods—Apollo in Greek mythology, Agni in Indian mythology, Tsontemoc in Aztec mythology, and Mithras in Persian mythology—all share long hair that extends in all directions. Ra of Egyptian mythology is also adorned with golden hair." (The Cultural History of Hair)

The gods reside within hair, and it contains the energy from the sun. The naming itself must be why I believe there is so much power within hair. If you use chemicals to change the color of hair, this energy immediately diminishes.

This force is so powerful that it outshines the energy of even the hairdresser when the customer enters the salon.

Consider fresh flowers and preserved flowers. Dried flowers are beautiful, but they do not have the strong energy and vitality of fresh flowers. People are the same way. Dyed, colored hair is not the same as natural hair. Nature is beautiful, and a god's creation should be kept in its original form. Vigorous energy comes with youth. Grace and dignity comes with age. I think this transition is a wonderful way of life.

The pursuit of artificial beauty, as in the case of preserved flowers, results in damaged hair, and the force of life diminishes. Fast and uncontrollable transformation from thinning hair to baldness is caused by the pursuit of chemical-driven beauty. Does this really make us happy?

We can obtain this result with a large investment, but I believe that investing in one's own growth is the best use of one's money.

Looking back in history, it seems that there has always been a desire to dye one's hair gray. In the late Heian Era (794-1185), the samurai Saito Sanemori is believed to have dyed his hair gray, fought hard and died in a battle. He was believed to be 73 at the time of his death. (Yamakawa Dictionary of Japanese History, Revised Edition, 2016, Yamakawa Shuppansha Publishing). According to "Miyako Fuzoku Kewai Den," written by Sayama Hanshichimaru, in the late Edo Era (1603-1868), black pomade made from walnuts, mulberry bark and pomegranate peel was used to make gray hair less noticeable by making it shiny. In the Ming Dynasty, people dyed their hair black with tannic acid and iron—the same substances with which women used to paint their teeth black—a process that took about 10 hours.

In foreign cultures such as the ancient Greek culture, it seems that there was a time when blonde hair was favored by young men and women. The comic playwright Menandros depicts a man who bleached his hair by sitting in the sun for hours on end after rubbing an ointment of ashes (alkali) hardened with beef tallow into it. This was said to be extremely damaging to the hair.

These people wanted to look young even if their hair got damaged. They wanted to follow the current trends. This desire is probably no different today.

We live in the 21st century. It's time that we begin thinking alternatively. If we choose to dye our gray hair, we should choose a method that is kind to both our health and nature.

"Nature is beautiful."

"Hair in its natural state is beautiful."

Now it is time we reaffirm these facts.

Hair
In Search of Natural Beauty

Contents

PART I

A Pitfall of Common Sense

Chapter 1

Traveling east and west to hand over 'beautiful hair'

100% natural henna does not dye gray hair black — A need to pass on the right information

Since 2009, I have held henna workshops throughout Japan. I travel to various locations every Monday, Tuesday and Wednesday, and work the remaining four days as a hairdresser at my salon, Kamidoko, in Tokyo's Minami-Aoyama district.

I began the workshop because the number of companies selling henna in Japan was increasing around 2005 and I was excited that people were finally learning about henna in Japan. However, the quality of henna sold on the market was declining, and consumers' complaints even reached the National Consumer Affairs Center.

The henna in question was either artificially colored to appear bright green, had chemicals added to dye the hair black, or contained almost no pigment, which is the active ingredient. People who used chemical-infused henna reported problems such as skin rash and swelling. Those who used henna that contained little or no coloring agents complained that they could not dye their gray hair black.

I was dumbfounded to hear about this because henna was just getting known and becoming more popular in Japan. This was around the year 2005.

In 1993, when henna was less known, I contributed a feature article in magazines and wrote a book to promote henna. Just when I thought it was finally becoming well known, the problem of altered, chemical-infused henna arose. I felt as if everything I had built up was crumbling. Some of the companies importing henna did not understand the original purpose and effects of henna or that artificial versions were being circulated in India.

Around that time, one of my clients who was promoting natural soap asked me to speak at an event organized by a co-op. I could feel the enthusiasm of the packed room and the response to my speech was very positive.

"We have finally understood the effects of henna."

After receiving many comments like this, I had several more chances to speak at these workshops held at the same venue in Tokyo and later in the neighboring prefecture of Kanagawa.

I have never sold my henna at these workshops. I was grateful for the opportunity to share "what is necessary and unnecessary for beautiful hair, as well as the benefits and roles of henna." I thought this was very important to convey.

Those who want henna at the event can purchase it (from other companies) through the Seikatsu Club Co-op if they choose to.

My experience as a lecturer has helped me realize that this method is actually very easy to understand. I continued to follow my concept of "Listen, read, understand, and put it into practice." Speaking at these workshops made me realize that writing the book did not waste my time.

When I told people that I wanted to hold a workshop, a woman who ran a yoga school in Suwa City, Nagano Prefecture, organized it for me. I discussed the concepts of "What is necessary and unnecessary to maintain beautiful hair," "Dissatisfaction with the quality of your hair is the greatest weapon to create beautiful hair," and "The conference that teaches you how to put an end to damaging your hair and aim for beautiful hair" at the workshop. After the talk, I'd respond to each participant's concerns as much as time allowed and give advice on how to regrow and repair hair so that it would be suited to their needs.

I wanted to see how the participants' hair would change over time. I asked the organizers if they could organize this workshop again in four months, and they readily agreed.

Of course, participation was not mandatory. Only those who felt inclined participated. I wanted to follow the process of how the hair actually changed and see how beautiful it became with natural coloring. This became a valuable experience and a great asset for me.

I did not receive any training or transportation fees from the organizers. I accepted anyone who was interested in participating in the workshop. This is how the Suwa workshop is now in its eleventh year as of 2020.

After Nagano, I was asked to hold the workshop in Asahikawa in the northern island of Hokkaido. Coincidentally, it was also organized by a yoga teacher.

Since yoga originates in ancient India and yoga instructors learn about henna at the beginning of their training, they are often active in promoting henna. Starting with 30 people, I have been able to observe changes in the hair of 400 people so far.

As the workshop participants' hair becomes more beautiful, they say people often ask them what kind of hair treatment or shampoo they use.

Receiving compliments for having beautiful hair boosts their confidence and helps cure what I call "the chemical hair coloring syndrome." The participants feel confident in their own natural beauty and feel that they no longer need to rely on chemicals to improve their appearance.

Having held a few workshops, I noticed that word was getting around. Now, people send me requests from across Japan; from the northern island of Hokkaido to the southern islands of the Kyushu region (i.e. Miyagi, Aichi, Mie, Gifu, Kyoto, Osaka, Fukui, Ishikawa, Niigata, Okayama, Kagawa, Fukuoka, Miyazaki).

The workshop is not meant to introduce henna products. Rather, it is meant to review hair care, to tell people that chemical-mixed henna not only damages hair but also causes hair loss. I also designed it to encourage people to inform people on what not to use, rather than marketing what to use. I try to tell them that the type of hair they were born with is the most suitable for their hairstyle and assist them with what is necessary to revive damaged hair. I also try to answer questions people may have about problems with their hair.

I talk about what genuine henna is, but never just about henna. Sometimes the conversation gets off-topic and fails to even get to henna.

I started the workshop because I wanted to let people know about genuine henna even though there is a trend to use chemical henna. However, once I actually started it, we've been focused more on what hair care to avoid to be able to maintain beautiful hair in a healthy way. Henna is certainly a very reliable remedy for restoring damaged hair, gray hair, and thinning hair.

I am sure that I will be able to fully reimburse my transportation and accommodation expenses for the workshops when people purchase henna products in the future. There are no guarantees, but I would like to imagine that this is the case. I've decided not to make the potential participants purchase henna before attending the workshop. Henna is truly effective only when people voluntarily seek to use it. I hope that those who believe in the benefits of using henna and feel the need to purchase it will do so voluntarily.

I have never started taking subscriptions. Once people sign up for regular orders, it is difficult for them to cancel their subscriptions. I didn't want to do that. Some henna sales companies sell henna through network marketing, but I do not want to conduct my business that way.

If you were born a giraffe, why did you become a zebra?
— Unexplained behavior of hair color enthusiasts

When I ask at the workshop if anyone has ever had a perm or their hair colored, most raise their hands.

When I ask why they did these things, they respond:

"Because it looks good," or "I thought I would look good with a perm."

When I ask, "Did you color your hair when you were born?"

They say, "No, I didn't."

"I was born a giraffe, and I have the body of a giraffe. But I long for the pattern of a zebra. I changed the pattern of my body to zebra stripes. I am now satisfied with my life.

But in a few months, the stripes begin to appear in blotches, just at the roots of the fur. I quickly color it again. I am back to having the body of a zebra.

I repeat this process and begin to think that I may not be a giraffe after all, but really a zebra.

Before long, I am totally confused. What am I?"

When I tell this story at the workshops, the expressions on people's faces gradually change. They begin to realize that it is unnatural to have their hair colored. When I talk about the color fading from the roots, they may recall their own experiences of saying, "I'm embarrassed to be walking around town like this." When we see our natural, undyed hair growing out at the root, we should feel the beauty of hair that has not had its melanin pigment destroyed. It is ridiculous that one would hate the natural, untransformed beauty of their own hair.

I tell stories as well about foreign artists who have undergone repeated plastic surgery. Most fans say that the artists looked better before they had the surgery.

Although the artists themselves may have been satisfied with what they did to their faces, people around them might have felt mentally trapped. I feel bad for the artists themselves, because their relatives and friends didn't like their natural appearance.

There is nothing more authentic than the way we came to life in this world, the way we were created. As important as it is to worry about the dangers of hair coloring chemicals, I think that it is more important to cherish the way we were born and the individuality we were born with. I hope that people realize this.

Some popular TV personalities and YouTubers have flashy coloring.

Many younger people admire them and dye their hair to be like them.

So what is individuality? I believe it is about making the most of one's innate characteristics.

TV talents and popular YouTubers have put their lives on the line to become what they are now. There is no need to emulate their behavior. What is left to imitate besides spending money and bullying your body?

People who say they have never colored their hair — Hairdressers do not explain enough about the treatment?!

When I ask workshop participants whether they have colored their hair before, most people raise their hands. Next, I ask if they have ever bleached their hair, and only two or three people raise their hands. When I explain that typically, hair is first bleached, and then color is added to it, they seem to get surprised. Many people think that hair coloring and bleaching are two different things.

In hair coloring, the cuticle is partially dissolved with chemicals, which then penetrate the cuticle and break down the melanin pigment in the hair, resulting in bleaching. When the original color of the hair is removed, the dye penetrates, oxidizes, and develops new color in the hair. During the coloring process, the hair is temporarily bleached and becomes gray.

This process helps explain how continued use of hair color can make hair more prone to graying (see pages 57~58 for details).

Hair coloring reduces the moisture content of healthy hair by 40%.

So it is inevitable that hair will dry out and get harder to arrange after repeated coloring.

I don't think hairdressers explain the hair coloring treatment process well enough before they begin.

Making the ivy stems more curly, stretching all the way to the other side — Perm makes hair unnatural

Think about curling the stems of an ivy plant in an unnatural way or straightening them out. Would it look beautiful? If the trees and plants in the forest had only straight branches, the forest would not be very interesting to look at. The world would be a boring place.

Not only is it boring to look at, but it loses its life energy when it is modified with chemicals. The very energy of the living being is lost. I feel it.

The same goes for hair. If we do unnatural things to our hair, its vitality will be lost. If you want to enjoy wavy hair, you can use hot curlers to curl your hair for the day. The heat from the hot curlers may not be good for the hair, but it does less damage than perms.

Have you ever had a hair stylist explain to you exactly what kind of stress you will be putting on your hair and body before they give you a perm? We encourage you to ask. Your hairdresser needs to explain to you exactly how it works.

Chemicals penetrate into the hair and deform the proteins when a perm is applied. The bonds between the proteins—the hair tissues—are separated and then rejoined in a different shape (in a bent state, since the hair is wound in bundles). This process creates waves, but it also damages the tissue. This process drains proteins and water from the hair, and it can cause various adverse effects (see page 80 for details).

It is important to remember that not only is the hair damaged, but the body is also exhausted by transdermal absorption. The same is true for hair coloring. Hair stylists should disclose negative information to customers and let them choose whether or not they would like to use the treatment.

Hair in its natural state is full of life — Chemical agents deplete energy

One day in 1988, I abandoned the idea of using chemicals on my hair. When I stopped perming and coloring my hair, the effect of the chemicals on my hair and how they drained the life out of the hair became clear.

Which do you feel more vitality and energy from, dried flowers or freshly cut/potted flowers? I feel more "life" from potted flowers and freshly cut flowers. Dried flowers are beautiful, but I don't feel any energy from them.

A beauty salon decorated with potted plants and cut flowers brings life to the empty space and creates an energetic and a vibrant atmosphere. A space surrounded by preserved flowers is beautiful, but it lacks vitality and life. That's how it is.

The chemically created preserved flowers are beautiful, but that's all they are. I feel that they are alien. I don't want to put something alien on the head of a living person because I think it will drastically reduce their vitality. I usually tell the people participating in the workshop this.

A hair rope woven in the Meiji Era, known as "*Kezuna*" is on display at Higashi-Honganji Temple in Kyoto. When I saw this artifact in the display case, I felt personally that there was strong energy coming from it. According to the explanation at the temple exhibition, women's hair and hemp were woven to make stronger ropes to transport giant timbers for reconstruction of the two halls at the temple between 1880 and 1895. This was a much-needed fix because the ropes kept breaking.

The 375-kilogram *Kezuna*, which was 69-meter long and 30-centimeter thick, was donated by a monk from Niigata Prefecture.

Hair is so strong when left in its natural state, but not when it is damaged by hair coloring. We can all easily imagine that. In our workshops, I sometimes cite historical episodes about hair like this one to show how strong and vital natural hair is.

How much more should we put up with when it stings — Risk of serious allergic reactions

When the hair begins to sting, the scalp is already under strain. However, many people can tolerate a little pain.

Customers do not think the chemicals used for hair are so problematic. They think that these chemicals are safe because professionals say so.

How much more should we put up with the stinging pain?

It is not something that we should endure. The chemicals used for hair can cause severe allergic reactions, breathing difficulties, and they can even be life-threatening. Please remember this when choosing a hair treatment.

Looking at the increasing number of color and perm treatments, it seems to me that many hair stylists are not very interested in learning about the ingredients of the chemicals. If they understood what they were doing, it is likely that they would choose different methods or stop the treatments. Perms and hair coloring are considered as a process to create a design (haircut), so more attention is paid to the perming techniques and coloring results than the possible side effects of the treatment. The stylists don't seem so interested in the associated risks.

Early on in my career in the beauty industry, I had a thought, which went something along these lines: "The more treatments I do, the more damage I cause to my clients' hair. Is it OK to continue this method. What causes this damage?" As I pondered this, I noticed that the plants in the beauty salon were losing their vitality. I wondered what the cause was. I also wondered if the permanent wave or hair colorant might have affected the plants. If plants and flowers ended up this way, not only the hair but also the human body would lose its vitality.

I have been advocating for about 30 years by now how unsafe permanent wave and hair coloring chemicals are. At the time, few people were discussing these dangers, and those that did were considered strange or suspicious.

Now, the government public relations agency as well as the Consumer Affairs Agency issue a warning about the dangers of hair coloring (see Appendix on pages 142~143) and post a warning on their websites that people with pre-existing kidney or blood diseases should not use hair coloring. The change has affected me as well.

Apparently, I am now perceived as someone who makes decent points about the health risks of perms and hair-coloring chemicals rather than a weirdo who complains about them.

The cost of going to a hair salon between the ages of 18 and 85 is 10 million yen — There must be more meaningful ways to spend money

"Have you ever wondered how much you pay for your beauty salon?" This is a question I always ask in the workshops.

The cost for hair care is much more than you expect. If you started hair coloring and perms after graduating from high school, the annual cost incurred between the ages of 18 to 85 would amount to 100,000 yen per year, or about 6.7 million yen for 67 years. If you included the cost of a wig you might purchase when your hair starts thinning, the total cost would be 10 million yen.

If you went to a hair salon once a month and paid 10,000 yen per visit, the total cost for a year would be 120,000 yen. The cost of going to a hair salon at this rate for 67 years until 85 would be 8.04 million yen. If the cost of a wig is included, it may amount to around 12 million yen. If you spend about 20,000 yen for hairstyling, the cost would be even higher.

The average price of a wig is about 500,000 yen, and some cost as much as 1 million yen. Considering that an average person purchases up to three wigs, it could cost about 3 million yen. One of the participants in my workshops spent 20 million yen on wigs alone. She liked to wear kimono and jewelry, and she bought wigs to go along with these items.

The growth of the business surrounding hair loss has been remarkable for the past few years. More advertisements for wigs and hair transplants are seen on TV and in magazines. Many companies are entering the market.

The cost of hairstyling can amount to 10 million yen total in one's lifetime. If we could spend this much money for something else, we could accomplish a lot. I think it would be more meaningful to invest this money into our self-growth or learning. If you can't think of anything in particular, you should try purchasing minerals, such as diamonds, which have a lot of metaphoric energy. People say wearing a real diamond helps you live longer. Jewish merchants historically wore emeralds, sapphires, rubies, etc., not to show off their wealth, but because they believed that the minerals brought them energy. Why not give yourself a necklace with a gemstone that gives you the power to live?

Hairstylist who gives you beautiful hair earns your trust — Beauty salons that increase treatments with use of chemicals and make profits go nowhere

In 2020, the government issued a request to stay home due to the coronavirus pandemic, which accelerated the transformation of the beauty industry.

In the past, we rarely saw reports about bankruptcies of beauty salons. Since the beginning of the pandemic, weekly newspapers and other publications have started to report on the issue. I talked about the increasing competitiveness of beauty salons for more than five years at my workshops. Historical data help explain this phenomenon.

In the coming age, only the genuine salons will survive. Hairstylists who think about the health of customers' hair and body will be the ones who can succeed despite the many challenges.

Perms, hair coloring, and treatments... If the salons try to make profit by increasing the amount of chemicals and contributing to destroying hair, they will surely fail as businesses because the public is now learning that these chemicals only result in short-lived beauty and cause more damage to the hair.

This is a problem not only for beauty salons. I think it is time for the patrons of hair salons to reevaluate their own hair and health, as well as the way they spend their money for their hair.

There are about 750,000 barbers and hairdressers in Japan (of which about 540,000 are hairdressers, according to the 2021 Ministry of Health, Labor and Welfare report).

I hope that the people who are planning to become hairdressers think about how to support the economy through their work.

Those who think about the economy and those who merely think about making beautiful designs will live completely different lives.

Stylists who become successful and open their own shops are almost certain to fail in getting their business off the ground if they only paid attention to design. They must think about health as well. When their business starts to suffer, their objectives as a hairdresser change. They trick you into believing that people think of you as unfashionable or sloppy if you don't get your haircut every month. They may apply hair coloring more than necessary, or color and perm on the same day. They become more focused on business and profit than style.

It is unfortunate that this happens, but these hairdressers are desperate to increase sales by performing more treatments, even if this involves destroying and repairing the hair. Before they know it, their goals have shifted from creating beautiful designs (haircuts) to pursuing treatments that increase sales.

This is also a problem for distributors of hair products. They sell equipment because it gives better results in perms and hair coloring. Such equipment is painfully expensive, but hairdressers think they have no choice but to purchase it.

Hair salons recommend the use of "nano mist" as well, claiming that it is effective by heating the hair with a warm mist. When we are given this treatment option, we should think about the risk of heating the hair during perms and hair coloring .The Japan Permanent Wave Solution Industry Association also urges caution regarding this procedure. Hair salons should also be aware of this (see page 142 of the document volume).

The economy is shrinking, and it is expected to get even tougher in the future. If salons continue to increase the use of chemicals to prioritize profits over customers, the customers will be the first to call out, "I can't spend any more money. I can't go to this hair salon anymore." Sooner or later, they will realize this.

To keep customers' hair both healthy and beautiful, we should not do anything that may be dangerous to our health. As the times we live in grow more difficult, it becomes more important for hairdressers to be considerate of their customers. Customers will leave behind a hairdresser who has no desire to change.

Sometimes even hairdressers attend my workshops.

I tell them from my experience as a hairdresser that "even if you stop offering perms and hair coloring, your clients will always appreciate your service and you can keep your business going because you give them really beautiful hair without perms and coloring."

If they choose to ask for advice from me, I take time to talk to them separately about how to manage a beauty salon that only offers treatment with henna and haircuts. My advice is based on specific data. Because they are giving up the main treatments provided by a hair salon, such as perms and hair coloring, sales are bound to decrease dramatically at first. But if they hang in there, there will be a way out.

Nutrition for hair comes from food, not treatments — Contradiction of eating pesticide-free vegetables and coloring hair

Many people who color their hair use treatments. It helps maintain the luster on hair immediately after coloring. It also preserves beauty temporarily, so people think that their hair is being nourished and restored.

Contrary to common belief, though, this is not the case. When hair is colored, 40% of moisture drains from the cuticle. To compensate for this, a treatment is applied. Hair treatments are highly moisturizing, attracting dirt and leading to more frequent washing. This then dries the scalp. The body thinks there is not enough oil on the scalp and tries to compensate by producing more oil. Pores are blocked. The consumer may end up seeking a more aggressive shampoo.

This is exactly the process that drives the economy of the hair care industry.

According to Yano Research Institute, the Japanese domestic hair care market is 452.75 billion yen by sales in the fiscal year 2019, up 100.9% from the previous year.

Although there was a slight drop in 2015, the market has continued to rise steadily each year to make up for it. The market for hair care products and hair transplants remains strong in 2019 as well. However, in 2020, the market is expected to show a decline due to preventative measures against the pandemic.

Use of moisturizing treatments to stabilize dryness can lead to problems such as sticky, heavy hair. People then use shampoos with strong cleansing power. This creates a negative trend. This habit of using treatments on damaged hair has become so ingrained that it is difficult to stop. What direction will this negative trend take when it is combined with the downturn of the industry in 2020?

As the idea to provide treatments is promoted and considered good for hair, even people with undamaged hair begin to use them in an attempt to preserve the beauty of the hair. We should not do anything unnecessary because it will destroy their beautiful hair.

Hair nourishment is best accomplished using a diet change, not a treatment. To restore hair, it is best to eat a well-balanced diet of protein, carbohydrates, fats, vitamins and minerals. Protein is what makes

Japan Hair Care Market Size

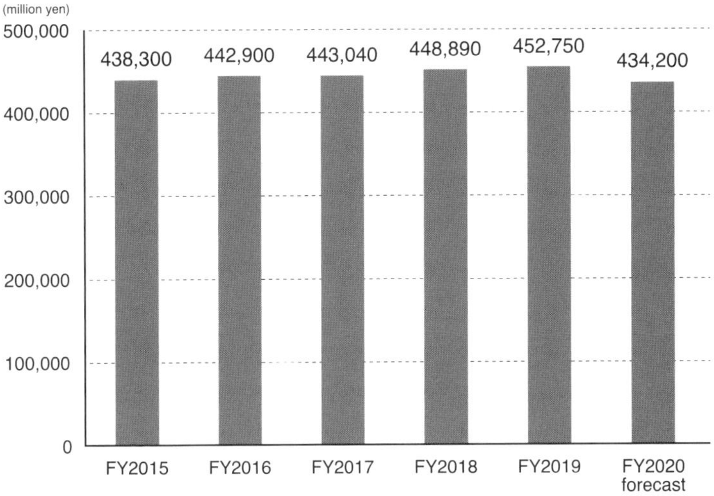

NOTE:
1. by sales
2. FY2020 shows a forecast.

*FY=fiscal year

Hair Care Market by Segment in FY2019

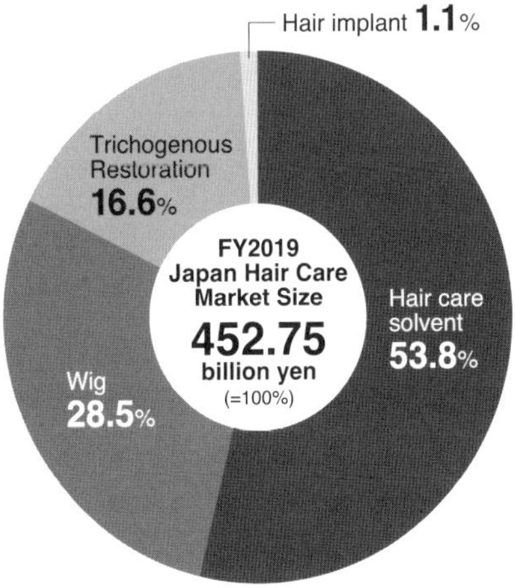

3. by sales
4. The wig market includes wigs, extension, restoration and trichogenous services as well as sales of such products, and hair care solvents include shampoos, conditioners and treatment.

Source:
"Research on Hair Care Market (2020)"
(released on November 9, 2020)
Yano Research Institute Ltd.

keratin, which makes hair. Zinc and vitamins are also important. Taking a large quantity of one nutrient can lead to a nutritional imbalance, so it is important to eat a variety of foods in a balanced manner. Many of the people who visit my hair salon are careful about what foods they eat. They are very knowledgeable about food.

"I only eat pesticide-free vegetables because I am worried about the harmful effects of chemicals," one client says. However, many of them dye their hair.

"What are you doing pouring pesticides on your head? Hair treatment products contain the same ingredients," I tell them. They look surprised upon hearing this.

"I never thought about my hair treatments. I only thought of them as part of my fashion statement." Interestingly, most people responded this way. For some reason, they were not as aware of the dangers of using hair care products.

Highly cleansing and moisturizing shampoos can upset the balance of the scalp
— Reviewing hair washing methods

When washing your hair every day becomes a habit, you feel like you have to do it. As the sebum is removed and the hair becomes dry, the body senses a need for oil and begins to produce more and more oil. As a result, the skin becomes greasy, and in severe cases, the hair becomes sticky. This not only forces us to shampoo our hair every day, but also leads us to seek out shampoos with stronger cleansing power. This is a negative trend, as mentioned earlier.

Let's look at other animals. They don't shampoo their hair every night.

Don't you wonder why only humans need to shampoo every day?

This is the kind of story we talk about in my workshops.

A veterinarian once told me that she sometimes receives dogs and cats that have scaly skin and coats from shampooing too frequently. When their owners stop shampooing and start washing only with hot water, their condition improves. One of the ingredients in shampoo, a chemical surfactant, washes away secretions from sebaceous glands, lowering the skin barrier and causing direct irritation on the skin. This causes inflammation of the skin.

Of course, not all skin problems are caused by shampoo, but they often improve when shampooing is stopped for a while.

Recently, more and more people are using only hot water to shower. Removing too much sebum using shampoo can be a problem, but it is necessary to remove dirt, excess sebum and oxidized sebum from the hair and scalp. Shampooing with hot water does not remove sebum easily and leaves excess sebum. If the oxidized sebum is not removed at all, it will block pores and lead to hair loss.

What if, then, we use soap? Pure soap leaves an oily, candle-like film on the hair. This film makes the hair sticky. Some people who wash their hair with soap may notice that their hair is sticky as if they have not washed it for days, even though they just washed it the day before. In addition, scalp and oily, moist hair creates an environment that is prone to bacterial growth. Soap dregs on the scalp and hair cause bacteria to multiply, making the hair not only unclean, but also smelly.

The other problem is the environmental issue associated with soap production. Soap is made from palm oil, which comes from the fruit and seeds of the oil palm-a plant native to West Africa. It is the world's cheapest and most widely used vegetable oil and is used in processed foods such as potato chips, instant noodles and ice cream. Japan alone consumes about 60,000 tons of vegetable oil a year. In 2015, most of the world's vegetable oil was produced from palm oil.

More specifically, the issue is environmental devastation caused by deforestation and changes in the ecosystem. Oil palms were brought from West Africa to Indonesia and Malaysia, where oil palm plantations were established. Since the 1970s, the area of land used for oil palm cultivation has rapidly expanded. Tropical forests are cleared and oil palms only are planted in place. At first glance, the plantation appears to be greener, but in reality, the ecosystem has collapsed and other organisms that cannot survive in this environment have taken over.

Human rights issues concerning workers on the plantations have also emerged. Lack of medical care and education for workers and their children as well as forced labor/child labor allegations have been reported.

Of course, there have been movements to curb the expansion of plantations and mend clear-cut forests in an effort to halt this destruction and preserve the environment to make the process more sustainable.

Japanese manufacturers of quality soap see this as an important issue and have joined the Roundtable for Sustainable Palm Oil (RSPO), an international non-profit organization dedicated to the sustainable production and use of palm oil, which addresses these environmental and labor issues.

When you think about how much soap we would need if we were to use soap to wash our hair as well, even more palm oil would be required. Soap is a necessity. The key to a sustainable world is to think carefully about when it's absolutely necessary to use some resources and where we can do without them.

I would recommend that people with healthy hair use a powder made from a mix of several herbs, which is dissolved before use. However, this powder is not suitable for damaged hair. Dry and unkempt hair requires a certain amount of moisturizing as well (see page 126 for details).

If you don't cut your hair for seven years, you'll have naturally beautiful hair — It requires time for all of women's hair to grow back

The amount of time that it takes for a full head of hair to be replaced is seven years for women and around four and a half years for men.

It is estimated that 70,000 to 150,000 hairs grow on a human scalp. Usually, two or three strands of hair grow out of each pore. After a certain period of time, the hair naturally falls out, and new hair grows back.

If a person with damaged hair does nothing for seven years, it will all fall out and a fresh batch will grow. If they did not perm or color their hair for seven years, all of their hair would be new and beautiful. The hair will change to reflect the person's characteristics. A hair grows 1.5

centimeters per month, or 126 centimeters in seven years. Theoretically, if no chemicals are applied for seven years, the hair will be completely restored.

Every time I return to Japan from India, I am more concerned about the broken hair of Japanese people. Indian women rarely change their hairstyles or cut their hair short. They only trim the ends of their hair. I think that such hair is truly beautiful and full of life.

Coating damaged hair with henna
— Waiting for new hair to grow while preparing the scalp

I look at the hair of all workshop participants and offer advice as much as possible. For those who already have beautiful hair, I tell them that they should keep it that way. For those with color-damaged hair, I tell them bluntly that they have a metaphorical rag on their head.

For those with damaged hair, I estimate that it will take three years to get it back to beautiful hair. Henna can help with that. You can even treat your hair with henna yourself. It is not difficult. Doing it yourself is more economical. Damaged hair cannot be restored, but henna coats it and stops moisture and protein from being drained. As the new hair grows over the course of three years, you can cut the damaged part off.

I ask the organizers to hold the workshop three times a year because I want to see the changes in the participants' hair. By having both first-timers and frequent participants in the same room, everyone will be able to see each other's hair and how it changed. Seeing is believing. If they see the change, it is more convincing.

My thoughts as a pharmacist

— After attending Mr. Morita's workshop
A pharmacist in Kitakyushu

Mr. Morita told us about a hair salon that has no choice but to retain its business by using hair colorants and perm products even if it knows they're damaging to hair.

"They sell their souls to work as hairdressers."

That's what Mr. Morita says.

The expression, "hairdressers who sell their souls," was shocking to me. It hit me as if someone had poured ice water down my back.

Mr. Morita said as he talked about his job as a pharmacist that he had many concerns. Some of them were along the lines of, If it were me, would I take this medicine?

Would I tell my family to take it?

I'm sometimes disgusted at myself handing patients prescribed drugs without hesitation.

Am I like the hairdresser who sells her soul to stay on the job?

It was with most of his questions and some of my own in mind that I headed home from his workshop.

"It is best to go to a hospital for treating thinning hair"

This became a household phrase. The Androgenic Hair Loss (AGA) treatment, which used to apply medicine to the scalp to induce hair growth, has now been replaced with internal medicine. This is good news for those who suffer from thinning hair, and I imagine they would be ecstatic when they see some results.

Both drugs, Propecia (introduced in 2005) and Zagallo (in 2006), suppress male hormones and extend the growth phase of the hair cycle, thereby improving thinning hair.

However, the warnings and instructions of the drugs contain the following statement:

Important precautions

- When this drug is administered to a pregnant woman, the development of the reproductive organs of the male fetus may be affected due to the pharmacological effects of this drug (DHT will be lowered).
- Pregnant or nursing women and women who may be pregnant or breast-feeding should not handle this product if it is split or broken. Handling broken pills can affect a male fetus. The active ingredient will be released when the outer coating is broken. It mentions the possibility of cracked pills affecting a fetus if pregnant women touched them. Although we are supposed to be able to avoid any effects to our health with the warnings and instructions of the drugs provided by the distributor. However, it implies that simply touching the drugs could cause some internal effect.

Although there is the benefit of improving thinning hair, there may be some unfortunate health effects for men. Side effects include decreased libido (<1-5%), erectile dysfunction, ejaculation disorders and decrease in the amount of semen (<1%). This is the flip side of having a perm or hair coloring. Even though you may be getting satisfaction from your appearance and fashion, you may be allowing harmful substances to permeate through your scalp.

Transdermal

At the workshop, some people said, "Shampoo and colorants are not absorbed by the body." I wonder if this belief is scientifically true. Tulobuterol patches that are often prescribed as cough medicine for children travel through the bloodstream very easily. (However, this is a drug designed to be easily absorbed, so it is quite different from shampoo in nature.)

Transdermal drugs are applied to the skin so that the active ingredients can be absorbed to the blood vessels and work on the whole body. They have been used for a wide variety of diseases, including Alzheimer's disease, cancer pain, hypertension, Parkinson's disease, schizophrenia and allergic rhinitis.

Transdermal absorbent has the following characteristics:

- easy use for children and the elderly who have difficulty with oral intake.
- a long life within the body and a very effective entry into the bloodstream as it does not pass through the liver
- The level of drug in the bloodstream is maintained while the patch is applied.
- A rash may be caused where it is applied.

The drug that touches the skin permeates and is activated on each and every cell of the body.

The skin is the largest organ of the human body, and effects of direct treatment through the skin are immeasurable.

Nature is beautiful

I am not denying the effectiveness or credibility of AGA treatment, perms or hair coloring. I just want people to know and understand the two sides to the treatments. We must think: Is there anything unnatural or unnecessary?

After meeting Mr. Morita, my awareness changed.

I am now aware of how beautiful nature is. The people who harvest henna, which is hard work, make it possible for us to have beautiful hair.

In the same way that our bodies are made by what we eat, what touches our skin every day has a great impact on us. Do you know where hair products come from and how they are made? As times change, we must question presented information and choose what decisions we make carefully.

Chapter 2
Beautiful hair and what destroys it

Hair is beautiful and unique
— Does the beauty industry cause headaches for some?

Bringing out one's individuality does not mean imitating the latest fashion or creating one's own trends with eccentric hair. If you can maintain the natural luster and tautness of your hair, as well as its color and waves, that is enough to make you shine. I have arrived at this conclusion after more than 20 years of working as a hairdresser and seeing many people's hair.

Beautiful hair is full of spirit or life force. You can see it in how shiny and strong the hair is. Shine and strength is guaranteed if there is a good balance between the level of moisture and oil in the hair. The proteins that make up the hair must also be undamaged.

The key is to have a clean and healthy scalp. Oxygen from the scalp and nutrients is as important as oxygen in the blood vessels in the body

When you fail to maintain a good diet, sleep well, or exercise, the amount of oxygen and nutrients absorbed through your blood vessels will fall out of balance. You start to have problems with your health. When you get your hair permed or colored, this destroys the proteins and causes your hair to have moisture imbalance. When you try to repair it with treatments, the moisturizing ingredients in the treatment products make the hair attract more dust and dirt. This, in turn, makes you want to wash your hair more frequently, disturbing the balance of the sebum film on the scalp.

Today, hair care at beauty salons seems to do things that are the opposite of maintaining beautiful hair. However, according to the Daijirin dictionary (3rd edition, Sanseido Books), a beauty salon is "an institution whose business is to beautify the appearance of women by giving perms, tying hair, applying makeup and performing other beauty treatments." According to this definition there should be no problem with a beauty salon declaring that it is a beauty salon even if it does the opposite of maintaining beautiful hair. In the definition, nothing is said about maintaining real, healthy beauty. People are attracted to artificial beauty such as dried flowers, not fresh flowers.

It is important to not overlook the fact that there is a problem with the way we take care of our hair that is causing thinning of hair. In the case of thinning hair, we are faced with a problem that could have been avoided if we took care of our natural beauty. I wish people would realize that the concept of hair color being more fashionable or stylish is nothing more than a commercialized impression.

Stop spending money on perms, coloring and unnecessary hair treatments. Rethink the way you wash your hair instead. We must not forget that washing hair alone is a very important issue, not only for the beauty of our hair, but also for our health, as well as the environment.

Preventing external shocks and expelling heavy metals and other substances from the body — The diverse roles of hair

As mentioned previously, hair is God. Hence, its role is important, and it is important not only for fashion. The hair growing in concentrated patches works similarly to a helmet, protecting the head from external shocks. It also prevents direct sunlight on the head and protects the brain from extreme heat or cold and also expels heavy metals—toxic substances-that have accumulated inside the body.

We can also gauge mineral balance and other parameters through observation of the hair follicles. We can even detect calcium and phosphorus, toxic heavy metals such as mercury and lead, determine gender, age, cause of alopecia (a hair loss condition), blood type, DNA and medical history among other information.

80% to 90% protein-hair grows on nutrients brought through capillaries — Understanding hair structure

A single piece of hair is composed of "the hair shaft," which is the part we call hair, and the "hair root," the part, which is inside the scalp.

The hair shaft is roughly divided into two parts; the medulla (hair medulla) and cortex (hair root), and cuticle (hair cortex).

The medulla is composed mainly of soft proteins. Most of its functions are still unknown. It can easily form cavities when exposed to external stimuli. When it gets hollow, light passing through is scattered, making the hair appear grayish and faded to the observer.

Composed mainly of keratin—a protein component bound by amino acids—cortex contains about 15% cystine, an amino acid-bound component. The cortex is a bundle of these fibers that accounts for 85~90% of the hair. It contains melanin pigment, which determines hair color, and CMC lipids, which maintain a constant moisture level in the hair.

The cuticle is the outermost layer and serves to protect the components of the hair. From the root to the tip of the hair, transparent cells overlap like fish scales to protect the hair from external stimuli. The cuticle overlaps neatly to create luster.

In the inner part of the scalp, there is an onion-like "hair bulb" at the base of the root, and inside that is the hair papilla. The papilla takes in nutrients brought by capillaries and sends them to the hair matrix cells in the hair bulb, which repeatedly divide and push up cells one after another for hairs to grow. Condition of the scalp greatly affects hair growth.

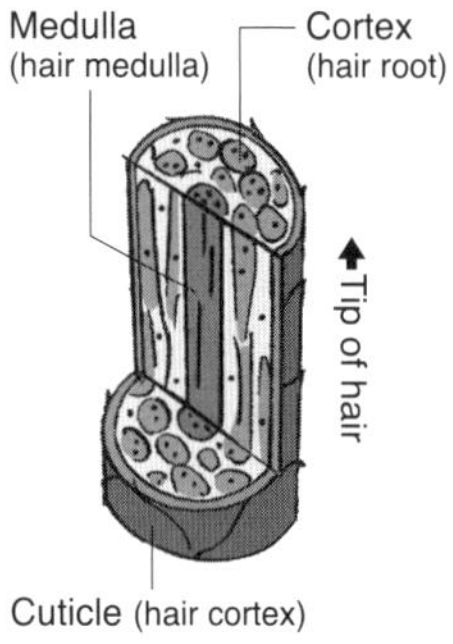

The ingredients in perms are also used in depilatories — These ingredients can trigger hair thinning

The perm agents break down the proteins that make up the hair and then bend (or straighten in the case of hair straightening) the hair to change its shape, before the proteins are joined again. They are also known as SS bonds because the parts where they bind look like two S's.

There are two types of perm solvents used in a hair treatment. The first one breaks the cystine SS bonds that hold together the fibrous bundles of cortices, which make up 90% of each strand of hair. Next, the second one binds the severed cystines together in twists to secure them in a wavy (or straightened) state. They are known as Type 1 and 2 products.

How many hairdressers explain the dangers of these products before treatment? How many of them ask about customers' health conditions and debate whether to continue with the treatment? How many inform the customers of the decision to continue or discontinue the treatment?

The first solvent is made by dissolving thioglycolic acid and other substances with an alkaline solvent. The second one is a solvent created by dissolving sodium bromate or hydrogen peroxide. In addition, a surfactant is required to mix the solvents into a cream. Surfactants used in hair products are synthetic, usually made from petroleum. These chemicals have the ability to break down the skin barrier, making it easier for the drug to enter the body. This process is quite dangerous.

If you are concerned about chemicals, please refer to the material data sheets and do your own research. You will be able to find important information that may otherwise go undiscussed this way. If you look the material data sheets up, you will learn that you may not be able to drink coffee or tea while getting a perm. You must avoid inhaling the vaporized chemicals through your mouth as much as possible.

Alkaline solvents and hydrogen peroxide are also used in hair coloring. This causes water and protein to drain from the hair, resulting in dryness. Hydrogen peroxide also destroys melanin pigmentation, causing hair to turn gray.

In addition, the following precautions are taken for heated two-bath type perm solvents: After applying the first solvent to the hair, do not expose it to a hair dryer, warmer, steamer, infrared rays, or any heat source. According to the "Voluntary Standards of Precautions for the Use of Permanent Wave Products" (revised on July 2002) of the Japan Permanent Wave Lotion Association, there is a risk of significantly damaging hair, breaking hair, causing skin damage, etc. from exposing hair to high temperature after a treatment.

However, many have experienced heat being applied by disk-shaped or rectangular machines, or warm mist being sprayed during a perm procedure. Why do hair salons do this, knowing that it is bad for the customer's health? The reason is because heating speeds up the penetration of the chemicals and reduces time required to complete a treatment. Efficiency is prioritized over avoiding dangerous processes. The warm nano-mist allows the chemicals to penetrate the hair very quickly, which means that transdermal absorption will be faster.

There are two types of hair stylists who use heating during perms. The first type just doesn't know the consequences of the treatments, and the other type are those who understand the possible damages and intentionally continue them in order to increase customer turnover and seek quick profit. The equipment they use is very expensive, and the price is a burden for their business. Ignorance and intentionally doing something wrong are both bad in their own ways. We must remember that there is not only damage to the hair. There are negative effects on people's health as well.

Coloring chemicals destroy melanin pigments — This results in gray hair

There are three main types of hair dyes: permanent hair dyes (quasi-drugs), semi-permanent dyes (cosmetics), and temporary dyes (cosmetics). Permanent hair dye includes hair colorants and gray hair dye. Semi-permanent dye includes hair glosses and glazes, and temporary dye includes hair colorant spray. I will explain the difference between quasi-drugs and cosmetics.

When you hear the words, "quasi-drug," "effective," and "hair dye containing active ingredients," you may feel that the product is good for your hair and that it is not harmful to your body. However, names can be deceiving. In the case of hair colorants, "effectiveness" refers to the effectiveness of the product in "hair dyeing," such as longer-lasting color or better color than cosmetics. It does not refer to health effects.

So-called "hair coloring" or "gray hair" involves mixing one or two solvents and applying them to the hair. Type 1 solvent is an oxidizing dye and alkali treatment solvent. Type 2 solvent is a mixture containing hydrogen peroxide, which is also an alkaline treatment agent. The oxidizing dyes used in Type 1 agents are para-phenylenediamine and para-aminophenol. The alkaline chemicals open the cuticle, making it easier for the dye to penetrate. Up to 6% hydrogen peroxide is approved for Type 2 solvent in Japan. It is dangerous to use more than 6%. Hydrogen peroxide decomposes and decolorizes melanin pigments, and oxidizing dyes in Type 1 solvent develop and fix the color.

When the alkaline solvent penetrates the cuticle, moisture and protein (keratin and cystine bound by amino acids) is removed from inside the cuticle, leaving the hair dry and damaged.

Since the core of the hair is lost, it is no surprise that we can't feel how strong our hair is anymore. This is a natural consequence.

Among the chemicals, the most common cause of allergic reactions is paraphenylenediamine (commonly known as PPD), an oxidizing dye used in Type 1 solvent. PPD not only damages the hair. It also causes pimples, swelling of the scalp, and even symptoms as extreme as swelling on the face, breathing difficulties. Please refer to pages 142~143 in this document for other symptoms, or the Japanese government's Consumer Affairs Agency's website.

Hydrogen peroxide, used in bleaching agents, not only destroys the melanin pigment in the hair and bleaches it, but it also destroys the enzyme tyrosinase, which is necessary for producing pigments. The more hair coloring is used, the more difficult it becomes to maintain hair color, and the more damage is done to the hair. You will have more gray hair after the treatments.

There are beauty salons that advertise "natural color; 96% organic." I would like you to ask the hairstylists who recommend 96% organic colorant what they use for the 4%. If the other 4% is hydrogen peroxide, for example, what is the point in even using natural color?

Cosmetic glosses and glazes coat the surface without bleaching — Problems happen with tar-based dyes

Are cosmetic semi-permanent hair dyes, hair glosses and glazes safe compared to quasi-drug permanent dyes such as hair color and gray hair dye? The answer is no.

The glosses and glazes are not like permanent hair dye, which uses chemicals to expand the cuticle and infuse the chemicals, destroy the melanin pigment and oxidize the dye to produce color. Semi-permanent dyeing is a method that coats the surface of the hair with color. Although less damaging to the hair than permanent hair dye, tar-based dyes such as Red 227, Yellow 203 and Blue 1 are known to be carcinogenic. If possible, it is best to avoid these dyes.

Some of the products are banned in Europe.

Treatments worsen damage — Destroying the good condition of the scalp

When I first started working as a hairdresser, I was concerned because the hair of the clients who got perms and colors was getting more and more damaged. I consulted with my senior. He said, “It’s all right. Don’t worry about it. There are treatments for these things.”

I tried to restore the damaged hair by using treatment products, but I wasn’t satisfied with the results. I thought it was a lost cause.

In retrospect, this was not surprising. The additives and coatings in the treatments temporarily add shine and texture to the hair. However, the hair itself is not restored. Instead, they worsen the condition of the scalp.

The moisturizers in the treatment products make the hair sticky and smelly, requiring frequent shampooing, because it gets easier for the hair to get dirty. Daily shampooing, in turn, removes too much oil from the scalp. Scalp with low sebum content is less able to protect the head from external stresses such as UV rays. If too much shampooing is done, the moisture in the scalp evaporates more than necessary. This is a common cause of scalp aging.

When the sebum film on the scalp gets out of balance, the body produces oil to compensate for it. The sebum film becomes thicker and clogs the pores as more is produced. This causes hair loss and frizz. The treatment is not productive. It is just an extra hassle.

The vicious cycle of hair treatment

1. You get treatment at a hair salon.
2. The strong effects of moisturizers in treatment products makes the hair sticky.
3. Shampooing is required more frequently as a result.
4. Too much oil is removed from the scalp by frequent shampooing, and no sebum film remains on the scalp.
5. Scalp is exposed to UV rays (which causes dryness and itchiness).
6. The body produces oil to compensate for drying of the scalp.
7. You tend to seek more powerful shampoos because of the extra oil produced.

Vicious Cycle

Chemicals for gray hair dye are a common service offered by beauty salons
— The first step to thinning hair is often a wig

When hair begins to gray, gray hairs appear evenly and gradually over the entire scalp due to aging. When gray hairs grow in concentrated areas, though, it may be a symptom of a hidden medical condition.

As a hairstylist, I come into contact often with my clients' hair, and I notice that there are characteristics in the way that gray hair grows. I've often wondered why gray hair grows the way it does, based on my observations. I met a researcher of eastern medicine named Toshiko Teruoka a while ago when I was wondering about gray hairs. About the same time that I met her, I learned that the location of concentrated gray hairs has something to do with physical ailments. Later, I learned more about this subject directly from Ms. Teruoka as we got to know each other.

When I ask the customers whose gray hair is concentrated in certain areas about their physical conditions, I tend to find that the gray hairs have something to do with their health.

When people go gray, they begin to color their hair to cover it up. As soon as gray hair starts to appear from the hairline, people start going to a hair salon. This works well for the hair salons. However, hair coloring and dyeing causes more and more gray hairs to appear. It also damages the hair and deteriorates the condition of the scalp. The hair starts to thin and balding starts, and you may soon need a wig. If these effects are actually the work of a hair salon, isn't the whole thing ironic?

Hair coloring and perms cause health problems — Mysteries of percutaneous absorption revealed

It was when I saw an article in the Asahi Shimbun newspaper on the morning of April 3, 1988, that I became fully convinced that hair coloring and perm chemicals damage the hair and also get absorbed through the scalp, which has negative health effects.

The article reported the results of a research project on the use of hair dye that causes aplastic anemia. Of the 960 patients, about 2%, or 19 of them, who had dyed their hair, had aplastic anemia because of something to do with the dye. When they were instructed to stop using hair dye or were treated for it, two healed and 14 had an improvement in their symptoms.

When I saw this article, I realized that my long-standing concern was, in fact, real. Hair coloring and perming solvents damage hair and also permeate through the scalp, causing adverse health effects.

The year 1988 was also when the first transdermal patch, known as "Adfeed" (and manufactured by Reed Chemical Co., Ltd.), which used a non-steroidal, anti-inflammatory drug, was introduced in Japan. This product started a trend in the use of drugs absorbed into the body through the skin.

In 1980, eight years prior, a salesman for a shampoo manufacturer showed me pictures and data that could be used to help detect a history of syphilis or other medical conditions from hair follicles. The photos were from the Metropolitan Police Department in the Japanese capital. He explained to me that hair follicles were used in police investigations. This was a year or two after I had graduated from beauticians' school and joined my first hair salon.

This was also around the time I began noticing the damage to my customers' hair due to perms and hair coloring. I imagined that the chemicals used in the perms and colorants could enter the bodies through the scalp. This would surely damage the customers' health and the hair also.

At that time, tests to measure body nutrient content balance through hair, which began in the U.S. in 1980, was not yet widespread in Japan. These tests determine what minerals you are lacking and help you keep a good balance between your nutrition/health and how many toxic substances you have accumulated into your body, such as mercury, arsenic and lead. Some of these are discharged from the hair. Hearing this fact, I thought, "It is likely that some of these substances enter the body through the scalp before they are expelled."

How could I prove this hypothesis? I started by researching various phenomena and gathering related materials. From that day on, I made sure to check with my clients about their health after they had received perms or hair coloring. I also read books and other materials on the subject. It was during this period of my life that I saw the article I discussed previously in the Asahi Shimbun newspaper.

I asked some colleagues who were senior to me about their opinion on the newspaper article. I asked them what they thought about the effects of hair coloring and perm chemicals on the hair and scalp. I was unable to get a clear answer or any thoughts out of them, though. Rather, I got the impression that they were not interested, actually.

I wanted to know the truth.

I decided to conduct thorough research on percutaneous absorption (substance absorption through the scalp) on my own.

Since ancient times, madder dye was said to be effective as an emmenagogue, depuration and anti-inflammation agent, and it was used for clothes that directly touched the skin, such as baby clothes and women's loincloths. In other words, people relied on percutaneous absorption for a long time before it was used for medical treatments.

I read more books and materials. I thought maybe I would have to study dermatology to learn more about percutaneous absorption. I never wanted to go to college so badly as I did then. But unfortunately, that was not financially feasible for me.

I was determined to learn on my own through books. Noticing that I was struggling, someone came to my rescue. One of my customers had studied at a university in the U.K. and had been working in the hair dye industry. He was very good at researching on the computer. He helped me find materials then, and again later on when I was researching henna as well.

The more we researched the chemicals used for perms and hair coloring, the more we found that they not only harm the hair but also our health. My belief that these chemicals are unacceptable grew even stronger. At the same time, a question arose between us. What was this business, really, where we were profiting from applying unhealthy perms and hair coloring?

We hold this illusion of instant beauty being a trait of a quality exhibited by fashionistas or sophisticated individuals, but our hair is only being damaged. Then we go to a hair salon to mend our damaged hair. The number of treatments we receive increases. The hair salon enjoys stable revenue as a result of this cycle. Hairstylists who are earning a stable income are also working in a dangerous environment where they are exposed to chemicals every day. Clearly, no one benefits from this cycle.

In 1988, I finally decided to stop having my hair permed or colored once and for all. In order to figure out what to do with my damaged hair now, I decided to turn to henna, which I began using in the mid-1980s.

When I first began to suspect that perms and hair coloring might not be good for my health, few people addressed the issue or even listened to me. Some people treated me as if I were crazy. Now, though, the Japanese government has even published an online article titled, "Beware of rashes caused by hair color! You can break out in allergic reactions. (2019)"

It also advises that anyone who has ever experienced a rash or itchiness from a hair coloring product (specifically in the case of permanent hair dye) should never use it again. People with kidney disease or blood disorders are also warned of the side effects, and those with scars or skin diseases are advised to avoid it. The government advises against using it during pregnancy, during recovery from illness, or when feeling unwell in general. When women are menstruating, they are also advised to avoid usage.

I wonder how many of you, as readers, have received such a warning at a hair salon before having your hair coloring done.

The dangers of gray hair dyes are often reported in weekly magazines. *Shukan Gendai* (May 5, 2018) published an article titled, "'Gray Hair Dye' Full of Hazardous Substances...! Japanese 'White Hair Dye' May Be Dangerous-Ingredients Banned Overseas Are Still in Use." The article said that chemical substances in the products "may cause liver disease or other health problems" and that the issue was also reported in

China, where "the main cause of chronic liver dysfunction over the past ten years was dye for gray hair. "

When I first became aware of the dangers of hair colorants in the late 1980s, we couldn't discuss the issues out loud for fear of being condemned for our beliefs. Times have certainly changed.

Since 2009, when we started holding full scale henna workshops, we have also talked about the effects of hair coloring chemicals on the liver. One time, a participant who had always been concerned about her mother's poor liver health told us after the workshop, "I'm going to ask my mother to stop dyeing her hair gray."

Four months later, she told us that her mother's liver condition improved.

Three years on, she went to the trouble to bring me the blood test data from the hospital, and I saw a real improvement in the figures. This is just one example, so I can't say for sure that the dye has negative effects on liver health for everyone. In any case, I am very happy to hear reports of health recovery.

When I first started the workshop, I sometimes had to begin explaining from the basics by discussing percutaneous absorption. These days, though, most people seem to know what it is. In terms of medical care, drugs using transdermal absorption such as ointments and nicotine patches are widely available and now known to the public. Currently, transdermal absorption is attracting attention in the field of nursing care as a way to help the elderly avoid aspiration pneumonia.

In 1967, RJ Feldmann published an article titled, "Percutaneous Absorption Rates of Topical Steroids by Site in Humans (Feldmann RJ, et al. J Invest Dermatol. 1967)," which stated that the scalp and forehead absorb better than the palms of the hands and soles of the feet. If the skin barrier has been disrupted or damaged by excessive use of petroleum-based surfactants, the absorption rate will become even higher.

I would like each one of you, as readers, to decide what you are going to do in the future after learning that the hair coloring and perms are damaging your hair and health.

Amount of transdermal absorption of steroids by body part (1967)

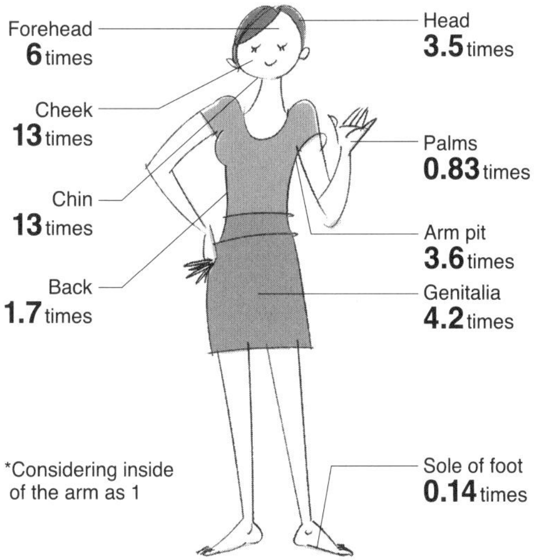

Chapter 3
The beauty industry that runs business in a vicious cycle

Japan's 250,000 beauty salons (as of 2019) — A number that is five times more than the number of convenience stores

As of 2019, there are approximately 250,000 beauty salons in Japan (Fiscal 2019 report of Ministry of Health, Labor and Welfare), an increase of 3,562 from the previous year. Tokyo alone has more than 20,000 salons. There are 4.5 times as many beauty salons as convenience stores (according to a 2019 report by the Japan Franchise Chain Association, the country has 55,688 convenience stores). It is no surprise that beauty salons are having a hard time surviving because of the coronavirus. Some have had to close temporarily due to the spread, while others have reported a 70% decrease in appointments. Their situation is growing dire as they must still pay rent and other fixed costs for their stores.

Actually, though, a sudden rise in beauty salon bankruptcies was present even before the pandemic.

In the fiscal year 2018, 105 beauty salons filed for bankruptcies, the highest number in a single year since 1989. The number of businesses that suspended or dissolved also increased to 317 in the same year, up from 264 the previous year. (Source: Tokyo Shoko Research)

In times of intense competition, managers are preoccupied with how to generate more profits. One way to do this is to recommend that:

- a haircut be done once a month;
- clients get hair coloring, perms and other treatments that use chemicals;
- and customers get treatment for damaged hair.

We'd ask, "Who damaged their hair in the first place to the point where it requires special treatments? It was the salons themselves, wasn't it?"

After recommending hair coloring and perms, the hairdressers at these salons never consider or mention the cause of the damage. Instead, they just recommend treatments to mend the damage. The hair only temporarily regains its shine and silkiness with the application of the treatment agent. Soon the skin starts to deteriorate, and the hair becomes more and more damaged. It then loses its shine.

The road to thinning hair and wigs

Looking stylish with trendy perms and hair coloring

Hmmm? My hair feels dry and messy. It seems like there are more split hairs as well.

My hair feels shiny once again after I color and perm it.

My hair is getting drier and now has more split ends. It also seems like more hair is falling out.

I got treatment at a hair salon, so everything is OK now.

Hair that has been damaged by coloring usually develops a detached cuticle and hollowing. The hair dye does not stay in this condition and easily fades. As a result, the customer ends up getting their hair colored more frequently. The amount of damage done by the treatment increases, and the treatment itself becomes essential. The cost of beauty inevitably continues to rise.

One month after the coloring treatment, hair in its natural color starts to grow back from the top area of the head. This starts the cycle of extensive damages to the hair occuring because more visits to the hair salon are encouraged. The damage increases further as hair coloring is applied more often. More treatment becomes necessary. Damaged hair fades faster, so visits to the salon become even more frequent.

When hair is damaged, some hairdressers only "pretend" to fix it. The fixing further damages the hair, and more treatments are applied to cover the damage. Gray-haired customers are welcomed at beauty salons because

I just went to a hair salon, but my hair already looks dry and messy. It feels like I've lost more hair.

I need to hurry to a hair salon to add volume to my hair with a parm and hide gray hair by coloring it.

This is strange. My scalp seems more exposed, and my hair is frizzled.

I must take good care of my hair by using hair growth agents.

I never imagined I'd need a wig one day...

the salons know that they will always come back to get their hair colored.

Perms and hair coloring never the same day — Has your hairdresser ever given you the right information?

If a hairdresser applies coloring and perms on the same day, it can be very dangerous.

The Japanese Pharmaceutical and Medical Device Act prohibits applications of perm and hair coloring at the same time, while the "voluntary standards of precautions for the use of perm and wave products (revised on July 13, 2002)" of the Japan Permanent Wave Industry Association (see pages 142~143) indicates there should be at least one week between the use of perm products and hair coloring.

Even if customers say they don't want to come back, potentially jeopardizing business, a hairdresser should still explain the procedure clearly. Granting customers' requests is not always in the best interest of the hairdresser. Fulfilling the customers' demands does not make a hairdresser kind. Doing everything that the customer wants to have done will only result in negative consequences in the long run. It is important to remember to keep the awareness and ambition of a professional hairdresser regardless of what the customer demands.

Customers don't know the health risks of hair coloring and perm chemicals. Even people who work in this profession and wish to make people's hair beautiful rather than make a profit become faced with financial difficulties. They are not sure what chemicals are harmful.

This is very unfortunate.

Some hairstylists listen to what the industry dealers say upon delivering beauty products and believe that hair coloring and perm solvents are not so dangerous. This is the reason why they are willing to give you more treatments. Hairdressers should study more on what they use.

Hair coloring and perm solvents can harm the environment — The dangers of pouring them down the drain

It is problematic that some people discharge chemical solvents into the sewage system without any concerns. In my book "Searching for Best Henna (Tsubanasha Publishing, 2017)," I had the opportunity to interview Dr. Masahiko Hirata of the Hirata Proctology Clinic in Tokyo's Minami Aoyama district about the health effects of chemical substances. He mentioned the problems associated with discharging hair colorants and perm solutions into the sewage system after use.

"If similar chemicals are used in the hospital, they wouldn't be allowed to pour them directly into the drainage system," he said.

Considering that toxic chemicals like these are poured down the drains of 250,000 beauty salons every day, I think this is extremely harsh on the environment. As Dr. Hirata added, because we do benefit from chemical substances, we cannot reduce them to zero. That is why we shouldn't use them more often than is necessary. In fact, it is better for our hair, scalp and body if we do not use them at all.

The Sustainable Development Goals (SDGs), which are set to achieve a sustainable society, were adopted at the United Nations Summit in 2015, and UN member states are committed to achieving these goals sometime between 2016 and 2030. Considering that there are guidelines set like Goal 12, "Ensure Sustainable Consumption and Production Patterns," and Goal 14, "Conserve and sustainably use the oceans, seas and marine resources for sustainable development," it is a serious problem that about 250,000 beauty salons in Japan are discharging large amounts of hair colorants and other chemicals daily into the sewage system.

Choosing not to color or perm your hair will break the negative cycle of using chemicals — Promised recovery even if we temporarily lose revenue

As for myself, in 1988, right after I decided not to offer any hair coloring or perm treatments, my business became very difficult to maintain. At the same time, though, I felt that I had no choice but to continue this path. In order to keep faith in my ideology, I worked part time in other businesses to compensate for the lack of income. Once I got over the difficult times, the path opened up.

Even after the pandemic, I enjoy a rise in the number of new customers, who have found us on the Internet during the stay-home period. We have not been doing anything spectacular, such as advertising extensively, but have only been doing straightforward, honest work. The work has borne fruit.

I always tell my regular customers that the less they come to the salon, the better it is for them. Even if they do not come to the salon for a while, I always give them tips on design and maintenance of their hair so that they do not have to worry about their hair being untidy.

Yet, some customers insist on coming to my salon, so I say, "You are not ready yet!"

This kind of conversation between me and my customers takes place often.

Changing the way we think can create a new vision for the future, which changes our customs. The future, then, will change much more than we originally expected.

Falling victim to the chemicals, a hairdresser leaves her job

— How one hairdresser became a henna specialist and restarted her career

A female hairdresser who worked at my beauty salon, Kamidoko, became independent in 2019 and opened her own hair salon specializing in cuts and henna.

She decided to come work for me because she noticed a change in her health. She had been working at a popular salon in Tokyo's Aoyama district for a year as a manager. One day, however, she developed eczema and black spots all over her body before she became physically and mentally ill. She ended up spending many days working at the salon off and on.

She could not talk to her father or brother, who were doctors, about her condition, because she knew they would give her a prescription medication. She wanted to avoid that. Unable to talk to anyone, she was tormented by the dilemma within herself.

She had a feeling somewhere in her mind that the chemicals used at the hair salon might be the cause of her physical ailments.

"In retrospect, I think my body and mind naturally rejected the drug. Even though I thought so, I was still confused because I couldn't organize my thoughts clearly."

She told me this.

She could not talk to anyone about it, so she did her own research. After going to a well-known dermatologist in Tokyo, she felt a little better. But as soon as she started working the rash came back.

Later, she turned to a homeopathy doctor-one who practiced alternative medicine-who pointed out that the cause of the health problem might be the chemicals used at the hair salon. She felt that her mind was finally at ease after someone, a doctor, confirmed what she had suspected for a long time.

Until then, she had become very sensitive to everything in her living space, including the air, sounds and smells. If she noticed even the slightest smell that did not physically agree with her, she would instantly become ill and collapse. Even the remedies prescribed by the homeopathic doctor were too sensitive and painful for her body to tolerate. After learning about the chemicals and avoiding them her symptoms began to improve little by little.

Since her homeopathic doctor was a customer at my salon, Kamidoko, he recommended for her to visit me. She started frequenting my hair salon to have henna done. There was another woman who was in charge of henna treatment at my salon at the time (she has now opened her own salon specializing in henna), so I don't remember much about the hairdresser who came to visit me. Within several visits to my shop, however, she wrote me a letter.

She wrote about how her health was deteriorating, how she thought the reason might be the chemicals used in the hair salon, and how she wanted to work at Kamidoko, my salon, because no chemicals were used there. When she was working at the previous salon, she thought that there might be a problem with the chemicals used for perms and hair coloring, but she was too busy with her daily work and immediate tasks to take the first step in seeking explanations to her concerns.

There are many hairdressers who have had the same experiences as her.

Salons destroy your hair with perms and hair color, make you think they can repair it with treatments, and then destroy it again. When you conduct a business with such a vicious cycle, it seems like there is no other way to success than that.

The current working conditions of the hair salon industry are such that they take away both time and energy to think.

An hourly wage for a beginning hairdresser might be as low as 390 yen. If they start perms and hair coloring at 7 p.m, which is typically the end of business hours, the last customer will be finished at 9 p.m. or even 10 p.m. After that, the hairdresser may start practicing and cleaning up. The next morning, they go to work at 8 a.m. If this way of life continues day to day, you may come to believe that this is the only way for a hairdresser to get their work done.

Let's get back to the hairdresser who was working at my salon.

I wrote a letter in response to hers saying that, "Unfortunately, I can only see risks when I consider hiring you, who spent 24 years at a hair salon doing hair coloring and perms. The shop is already well run with the current staff. It would only have a negative effect on the shop's finances if I had to prepare to pay you. However, I think it would be an interesting experiment. Some of the hairdressers who have participated in my workshops have said at least once that they would give up hair coloring and perms. After a while, though, they go right back to their routines. They must continue to stabilize their business, they say. I think it would be an interesting challenge for me to see if you can restart and survive as a hairstylist who only offers henna and cuts."

I told her this as a response to her letter that showed strong commitment to work for my salon.

"If you stay here forever, I'd lose my objective in life and my business plans. So, why don't you aim to become independent in three years and commit yourself to working everyday in the meantime? That would be a good compromise."

These were the conditions of employment that I set before her.

I thought that many of her potential customers would be likely to have had their hair colored or permed before. She would receive various types of customers, such as those who just want a cut, those who want henna done and a cut, and those who have had their hair colored or permed but want to have henna applied to their hair. How would they react if we tell them we only offer a cut, or henna and a cut as a service? I felt that this was a good opportunity to experience such things firsthand.

Fortunately, one of her old clients told us her hair became more beautiful since she received treatment at my shop. "I'm glad I came here," she said. The new business idea was very successful.

At a major hair salon in Tokyo's Aoyama district where she worked, she also offered henna treatment. However, she said that the feel of henna was quite different from the Lakshmi variety. I was glad the clients seemed to feel a difference in the quality of our henna.

I told customers from the beginning that all her current clients should go to her store when she decides to quit my shop in the future. That way, she would be able to expect a good number of customers from the start of her independent career. I told her everything about how to start the business and how to manage it.

She became independent in three years as promised. Now, looking at how she purchases her henna, it is clear that she is very committed to specializing in henna and cutting hair.

I think the economy will decline soon. If we continue to run our businesses based on perms and hair coloring as we have in the past, we will probably not do well. We need to think about how we can serve our customers best.

We need to think about coexistence with our customers. We need to run a business that pursues beautiful hair without putting a burden on one's health and without damaging the hair.

When a hairstylist who has managed a hair salon that provides hair coloring and perms, decides to run a salon specializing only in henna and cutting, the business will be difficult at first. The mainstay of the business, hair coloring and perms, is no longer bringing in any profit. Faced with the harshness of the business, many stop pursuing their ideals. We must not waver in our determination to do only henna and cuts. If we hold on to our ideology, the number of customers we receive will surely increase. People whose hair became beautiful because of healthy treatments will naturally attract more people who are interested.

PART II

Treat Your Hair Like It's Your Client

Chapter 1
Days at Kamidoko Beauty Salon

Bringing back beautiful hair in three years — Using the power of henna to cure damage

For first-time customers with damaged hair, the first step is to talk about how we can restore their hair.

When coloring is done frequently, the body reacts to foreign substances entering the pores, which then shut down. The scalp stiffens accordingly. The amount of moisture and protein in the hair is also reduced, resulting in frizzy, coarse dry hair.

"Your hair will recover in three years after you stop coloring it," I tell my clients.

If you can't picture the results of your effort, you may feel uncertain about working on your goals. But if you can see the goal three years down the road, you will most likely try to do your best.

Of course, at the very least, we should explain to the customer why the hair is damaged. I tell them, "We will cut your hair in a few months. Then in a few years, you will have more new growth and your naturally beautiful hair will come back. When your natural hair grows back, I'll see how we can cut it in a way that will be more manageable. I'll 'talk' to your hair."

I decide what to do based on the condition of each customer's hair. I may cut the damaged hair and make it short. Or, if the hair looks like it won't get any better with a medium length cut, I'd tell the customer to leave without doing anything because it would be a waste of money. Of course, I don't charge a fee if no treatments are done. I just tell them when to come back next.

"I want you to treat your hair with henna once a week by yourself," I tell my clients. "If you use henna to take care of your damaged hair while also caring for the scalp, healthy new hair will grow back."

I describe the effects of henna on the hair and how to continue henna treatments at home.

I'm sure the number of people who went home after a quick chat with a hairstylist without receiving any hair care was not many. Still, I'd often have this exchange with my customers.

You can ask me as many questions as you like until you are satisfied. If you are convinced with my explanation and practice what I explain, your hair will grow back quickly. I believe that the henna plant is responding to our commitment in a way.

When my clients receive compliments on how beautiful their hair has become recently, it encourages them to continue with the henna treatment at home.

"I listen to what the hair wants before I ask what my clients want. I treat the hair itself like it's my client." If you don't have this kind of attitude, you cannot truly touch your customer's heart. Even if I am that sincere, I still have some people come to tell me, "I'm sorry, but I colored my hair."

If that is the case, it is fine. They can go their separate ways. But if they say, "After I colored my hair, it was damaged, and I regret it. So please give me the henna treatment again. I want to make my hair beautiful and healthy."

I suffer a great sense of loss when my clients tell me that. I make a schedule at the beginning of the henna treatments for beautifying the hair. I create a long-term plan that includes a number of different cuts to try at different intervals for me to see the characteristics of the customer's hair and get a general idea of the final design. Gradually, the condition of the hair improves and the beautiful new hair that is finally free from any chemicals is growing.

But just when I think I have it all figured out... I discover these clients using chemicals on their hair. Then everything goes back to zero. We have to start all over again.

Even the beautiful hair that grows back has destroyed melanin due to hair coloring, with protein and water drained from the hair. Nothing could be more devastating.

I was surprised when the proprietress of my favorite soba noodle shop showed me her colored hair after it had regained its beauty.

She said, "One of my customers was a young hairdresser who just started working, and she begged me to get my hair colored."

When I heard this, I thought the proprietress was being kind to her regular customers. That was good. However, all my energy was drained.

Damaged hair does not recur. Hair doesn't hurt or bleed. That's why we fail to take it seriously enough. Henna is a first aid treatment for damaged hair, which prevents the loss of moisture, protein and shine. It improves the health of the scalp and helps newly growing hair keep good health.

Although henna is applied to damaged parts of hair to temporarily repair the cuticle, the destruction of melanin pigment cannot be reversed. It takes a long time to restore the hair to its natural beauty. If hair coloring or perming agents are applied in the middle of this process, you must start all over again.

One of the reasons many people come to my salon is because they see how beautiful their acquaintances' hair has become. They think, "If my hair becomes this beautiful again, I would like to go there too."

I want them to ask me about hair coloring, henna, hair care and anything else they wonder about. I will be happy to answer their questions. Once the questions are answered, I want them to follow my "plan to bring back beautiful hair" and stick to it. The more obedient the customer is with this plan, the faster their hair will become beautiful.

There is no need for a monthly haircut — What I tell people with beautiful hair

Although there are only a few of them now, we occasionally meet customers with beautiful hair who have never had their hair colored or permed. Many of them come to me so they don't have to keep declining offers at other salons to color or perm their hair.

There is one thing I tell people with beautiful hair.

"You don't need to go to a hair salon once a month."

Many people believe they should at least come once a month for a cut. That is not true; even once every two months is too much. For long hair, once every six months is fine.

"For the 6,000 yen you may have had to spend for your hair cut, you can instead enjoy a more gorgeous lunch and go to an art museum before heading home. There are museums and good lunches in Aoyama," I tell them. "In this condition, you won't need another hair cut for another three months."

Examining the condition of my clients' hair, I tell them this. The key is to change this mindset of going to the hair salon once a month first.

Styling changes with hair bring out one's charm — Respect one's personality, and make it shine

Hairdressers often try to make customer's wishes for their hair styling come true but fail to do so successfully. Or, the haircut ends in success, but it is out of sync with the clients' character.

Some clients, as soon as they sit down in the chair, start talking about what they dislike regarding the quality of their hair. There is a surprisingly large number of them. After a brief discussion, they talk about what kind of hairstyle they are hoping to get. They start talking about what they want to have their ideal hairstyle look like. But it is always difficult to determine whether the hairstyle they wish for will look good considering the quality of their hair.

Some hairdressers try to create the haircut the customers want by using whatever techniques they can, even if it damages the hair because they want to try to live up to the customers' request.

However, hair modifications done in this way end up making the customers look awkward because they cannot look at themselves truthfully and see what looks best on them.

Instead of forcing the hair to change, I have a conversation with it. I look at the quality of the hair and think about how to cut it. "Cutting hair" does not mean cutting it off. Rather, it is to rearrange and arrange the hair to make it look beautiful. I respect the personality of each person's hair. Most people will realize that what they thought they dislike about their hair is in fact their individuality. They also learn to realize that it is this individuality that makes their hair more attractive.

People with curly hair want straight hair, and people with straight hair want wavy hair. Rather than yearning for what you don't have, it is best to use what you do have to your advantage. By taking advantage of a person's unique individuality, and by using a good cut that takes advantage of the natural waves and curls, a hairstyle that is more appealing can be created. If the hair is very curly and difficult to manage, continuing to use henna will help create just the right amount of wave and make it manageable.

The hairdresser's job is to understand the person's hair quality and give them a haircut they can be proud of, rather than just answering to the consumers' demands. Customers will learn that the hair quality and frizzy hair that they used to dislike can be turned into their charms. They will come to love their own hair. This is what I believe is the true work of a hairstylist.

Scissor marks can be used to tell hairdressers' technique — The cuts are what make the difference

The quality of a haircut depends on the quality of the blade and the direction of the scissors and the speed in which they run through hair. This greatly affects not only the condition of the hair itself, but also the durability and longevity of the hairstyle.

The "consciousness" of the individual hairdresser is also important. I cut hair while thinking about hair arrangement. When I cut hair with the final design in mind, the hair becomes more manageable. Hair is delicate and very difficult to handle.

A hairdresser who takes good care of the blade is also a good cutter. The hair changes its feel to the touch depending on the cut. The most skilled hairdressers cut the hair at 90-degree angles with sharp scissors. The cross section is minimized, and the loss of protein and water is kept to a minimum. Cutting hair with scissors that do not cut well will result in split ends immediately after the cut. Imagine cutting a piece of string with a pair of scissors that don't cut well. The same concept is true with hair. Your hair will split, and you will have split ends immediately after the cut.

"At the end of the day, always wipe the blades, the edges, and the screw threads with chamois or similar material to ensure 100% performance at all times."

This is what a salesman at a specialty store for scissors once told me. He said that those who do this are hairdressers who have a good relationship with their scissors. On the contrary, he said that it makes him sad when he sees scissors full of hair.

Hairdressers, who take good care of their combs, hair dryers, and other tools, and see the importance of hygiene, are excellent hairdressers, both from the hairdresser's point of view and from the tool specialist's.

An expert on scissors said that when he looked at some scissors before sharpening, he saw some naturally worn out without major dents in the blade while others have major dents in some places. Naturally worn scissors are a sign of good quality work. Since they are supposed to be used for cutting at one-third the length of the edge, he thinks that there is a lack of skill on the part of the hairdresser when he spots them with a lot of wear at the base of the blade.

There are some hairdressers who do not polish, sharpen or maintain their scissors very much. When we asked an expert how often we should sharpen them, he replied, "It's difficult to say how much because we cut many different types of hair, ranging from clients with stiff hair to those with soft hair. Each hairdresser should know when they are in their best physical condition, as well as when there is a change in their condition through hand or arm fatigue, etc. When they notice wear on the scissors because of their tiredness, it's time for sharpening."

According to the data gathered by sales departments, scissors need maintenance when they have cut the hair of about 300 people.

I use three types of scissors. The brown cut, in which the scissors are placed at a 90-degree angle, is my main cut. The same brown cut can vary depending on the person's hair quality. That is why I use different types of scissors depending on the hair type of the client.

By cutting at a 90-degree angle, haircuts can be minimized. The loss of water and protein out of the cut is also minimized. This is why the brown cut is the cut of choice for me.

There is a sharpening method that's appropriate for each cutting method. For the stroke cut, the scissors cut from the tips of the hair toward the roots, and for the brown cut, they are placed at a right angle to the hair. No hairdresser uses the same scissors for all cuts. Because the scissors are expensive, we consider them a big investment. However, the investment makes sense because it is essential.

I even make an original handle for my own scissors so that they fit in my hand. This allows me to put all I have into the work. I send out the scissors for service on a regular basis.

If you want to find a hairdresser you can trust in your local area, it is important to know if they take good care of their tools. You can tell how skilled they are based on the condition of their equipment.

Chapter 2
30 years of working with henna

Henna, a plant that even Cleopatra loved in ancient times — What is henna?

The scientific name of the plant known as henna in Japan is Lawsonia inermis, and it originates in India, Nepal, Sri Lanka, Pakistan, Iran and other Southwest Asian countries, as well as Egypt and Morocco. It is also known by its Japanese name, Shikoka or Tsumakurenai-noki.

Henna is a three- to six-meter shrub with spreading branches and leaves that produce small cream-colored flowers and blue-black fruits with a strong smell. The leaves make red dye that is used for body painting, known as henna tattoos, and for dyeing hair, nails and fabrics. It is sometimes used to dye the manes of Arabian white horses.

Traditionally, used in the subtropical regions of the Middle East, Asia and Africa, henna was brought to different parts of the world by immigrants. It is used for traditional body decoration and also plays an important role in religious wedding ceremonies. It was also believed to have healing effects.

In "burials of the ancient Egyptians" (written by Koichiro Wada, published by Poplar Publishing Co. in 2014), it is described as follows:

> The mummies underwent elaborate cosmetic transformation . First, eyebrows were drawn, gray hair was dyed with henna (a vegetable dye), hair was trimmed, and a wig was applied to areas where hair was thinning.

The reason why some mummies' hair remains strong today is probably because they had healthy hair to begin with, having never been permed or colored. It was also coated with henna.

When mummies were processed, the bandages were dyed with henna because it contains naphthoquinone, which is said to protect against fungi and mold.

Henna blooms in the field in Rajasthan, India.

Even today, women in the Tarai regions of India and Nepal decorate their hands and feet with beautiful art painted in henna during weddings and other festive occasions. Hindus believe that henna is a plant highly favored by Lakshmi, the goddess of wealth and good fortune.

Henna from Rajasthan, India, is high quality — Henna in hair care

Henna as a hair-care product is made using henna leaves harvested in the fall, which are dried and ground into powder. Only young leaves make good quality henna.

Most henna used in Japan comes from the Indian state of Rajasthan, where the best quality henna is harvested. Henna is mostly grown in Rajasthan and Gujrat. Rajasthan is located in the desert region of India, where the average mid-day temperature exceeds 40 degrees Celsius and the night temperature drops to 10 degrees Celsius. Rainfall is minimal and humidity is low. This harsh environment provides a good location for henna to grow.

Knowing the positive effect, we order more than 100 kinds of henna from all over the world — My first encounter with henna

In 1984, the first store I rented when I started my own business was "Atelier Shin," which was run by Shin Yoshino, the artistic director of Vidal Sassoon. Based in New York City at the time, Yoshino only occasionally returned to Japan. There was henna left in the store, and it was purchased in the U.S.

What is henna?

When I first tried it, I felt a positive effect, although it didn't work well in hair coloring.

That was where my research began. I contacted my aunt, who was living in New York at the time, and told her about henna. She then sent me all the different kinds of henna available from the manufacturer who made the henna that I'd found in the store.

I asked my friend who is fluent in foreign languages to gather documents on henna and to order it from various countries. I was able to acquire samples of henna from more than 100 companies in places such as the continent of Africa, India, Australia and Yemen.

We found that particles of each henna powder differ in size, color, aroma and taste. I got a rash and blisters, as well as an acute sensation from a clearly dangerous smell, from them.

I felt urgent to find out if there were any radioactive materials in the product, so I asked my brother, who works in the quality control office of a long-established beverage company, for advice.

When I saw products with the names "barium oxide" and "para-phenylenediamine" on the ingredients label, I wondered if they were drugs and thought about ordering some samples. So I asked my brother about it, and he said that these were dangerous drugs, not something a private citizen would order. I felt then that I would be in trouble if I did not use safe and healthy hair products for treatments. .

When I first started my own store and found henna (1984~1987), I was still doing perms and hair coloring. I tried many things to see if I could somehow repair the damage to my hair caused by treatments. None of the methods had good results, so I began to focus more on researching henna.

After moving to Tokyo's Kita-Aoyama area in 1987, I continued to offer perms and hair coloring. There, I discovered from my observations that the more frequently people had their hair permed or colored, the more severely their hair was damaged. Treatments did nothing to improve the damage. They only seemed to make the hair temporarily beautiful and further damage it.

I was uncertain about what the results would be but wanted to see if henna would work. I told potential clients that henna could be expected to keep their hair beautiful but that I was still in the experimental stage, unsure of what would happen still. I began treating those who agreed to henna treatment free of charge.

When some henna takes effect, it turns gray hair black or unnaturally dark. Some customers complained about this effect by saying, "I can't have this color." I never forget how surprised and sorry I felt when I saw their reactions.

Most people who colored their hair those days did so to dye their gray hair black. During the "bubble economy" (1985-91), Japan's period of economic growth, the trend was to have black hair and thick eyebrows. It was not until after the bubble economy burst in the early 1990s that young people began to dye their hair in various colors as they do now.

Coloring was popular among young people during the recession prior to the bubble economy. It seems to me as though people wanted to dye their hair in other colors because of the recession.

Some say that the hair color trend among young people in the 1990s was largely influenced by the fashion of popular singer-dancer Namie Amuro. TV programs and commercials were very influential in spreading this trend.

While henna treatment was offered to some customers free of charge at my salon as a way to show its effectiveness, I still did perms and hair coloring. I would destroy the hair with these processes, patch it up with treatments and repeat perms and hair coloring yet again, which further destroyed the hair. I knew that the chemicals were not good for my health, but without any conclusive evidence, I could not successfully make the decision to stop chemical-based treatments. On April 3, 1988, an article in the morning edition of the Asahi Shimbun newspaper caught my eyes. It talked about how transdermal absorption, particularly hair dyes, might be causing aplastic anemia (see page 62).

How media reports on transdermal absorption led me to change my beauty salon so that it specialized in haircuts and henna only. — Focusing on promoting henna

I felt the negative effects on my health. I decided to abandon hair coloring and perms.

When I told my clients about it, they said they couldn't agree to suddenly suspend these services.

My clients said things like, "You've been coloring and perming my hair knowing that they are bad for my health?" "I like my perm," or "I like my color."

I received more rebuttals and comments of disapproval than I expected.

There was a family of four who had been coming to my salon for a long time. When I told them that we would suspend the perm and color services, they all moved to another salon.

Changing our specialties was something I had been thinking about for a long time, but for my clients the announcement came suddenly and unexpectedly. It was inevitable that they complained. I felt guilty, as if I had betrayed them. I explained to them that chemical hair coloring and perms were not good for their hair. They still left, and my sales dropped by about 30%.

Still, that did not make me want to resume hair coloring or perms. I decided to take measures to cope with decreasing sales by cutting costs and taking on a second job.

In the midst of the bubble economy, we were evicted from our salon in Kita-Aoyama due to new developments taking place in the area. The rent for the new location was very expensive. I figured that the bubble economy would not last long and decided to cut costs as soon as possible. When the bubble economy burst and a recession followed, I felt relieved that I had made the right decision.

We believe in "not destroying hair, not damaging healthy hair, but instead maximizing the beauty of natural hair."

Some clients, in fact, came back to Kamidoko. One such customer is the daughter of the family of four that left Kamidoko. She, as well as others who returned, are the driving force for me to continue my work the way I want to. I am very grateful for that.

What do we do with damaged hair—?

We begin by explaining henna to customers suffering from damaged or thinning hair and offering henna treatment to those who agree to it. We have been giving free henna treatments to our customers for a long time, and they have been fully aware of the benefits of henna. I stopped offering perms and hair coloring altogether and began advertising my hair salon as one specializing in haircut and henna. I eventually began charging a fee for henna treatment.

I purchased 100% plant-based natural henna from a Japanese supplier at 40,000 yen per kilogram (at the time). The price of "Organic hair color: Orange," a product we currently sell, is 1,800 yen (excluding tax) for 100 grams. In comparison to 18,000 yen per kilogram, 40,000 yen seemed quite expensive, but since this was the only wholesaler in Japan at the time that handled 100% natural henna, we had no choice.

Henna was originally imported as "miscellaneous goods." It was not until the Pharmaceutical Affairs Law was revised in 2001 that henna started to be marketed and imported as a "cosmetic product." In order to sell henna as cosmetics, it is necessary to apply for and obtain a license from the health and safety department of a local government (in the case of Tokyo, it is the Tokyo Metropolitan Health Safety Research Center). However, this was not necessary when henna was considered a "miscellaneous good" instead of a cosmetic product.

What should I do to raise awareness about henna so that more people can use it?

In 1993, I pitched a feature story proposal with "Shinbiyo" (Shinbiyo Publishing, now called "Shinbiyo"), a magazine for the beauty industry, to publish the information I had obtained through my research, as well as the process and the results of practicing henna treatment on my customers. In 1993, my proposal made it into the magazine as a special feature on henna, and the response was even greater than expected. So they decided to launch a program called "Henna Study Group." About 100 people from beauty salons all over Japan gathered to join the group.

In 1995, apart from the group and my salon, I established a company called Lakshmi to sell henna. We decided to do business directly with Indian henna manufacturers, so we ordered samples from companies dealing with 100% plant-based henna and selected the best kind.

Having used henna, I was able to move away from "hair-damaging treatments." Furthermore, henna also helped repair damaged hair and improve graying and thinning of hair. In fact, my henna customers have expressed their delight about my decision to switch.

In 1998, I wrote a book about henna called, "Treatment Color Henna" (Gakuyo Shuppan Publishing), to convey my feelings on the subject and document my experience properly.

A decision to discontinue production of henna in gel form for easy use — Delivering safe and effective henna, not what the times demand

Many customers said that dissolving henna powder was hard to do at home.

In order to solve this problem, we took the imported henna powder to a Japanese cosmetic company and commercialized it, marketing it as henna gel.

In 2000, we began selling a henna gel called, "Lakshmi Hair Color Treatment R," for 2,400 yen (without tax). It was just enough for approximately two treatments. The gel form is moist, which makes it easy for bacteria to multiply. We sterilized the product with gamma rays to prevent further bacterial growth.

The product was a big hit, and we updated it in 2003. However, after one year of production and sales, it was found that the product failed to dye the hair completely. Close examinations revealed that the amount of naphthoquinone, also known as Lawsone, a pigment component in henna, decreased due to the effects of gamma ray sterilization.

It sold more than 10,000 bottles a year and was the lifeline of the company, but it became more difficult to sell them for it was no longer effective as a treatment or dye. If we continued to sell a dye that was no longer effective as a treatment or dye, it would go against my personal aspiration to "work to make hair beautiful."

The suppliers were strongly against suspending sales of the product. Since the product has a three-year shelf life and the amount of Lawsone only decreases after one year, we decided to continue selling the stock for at most one year. The people who purchase the product will typically use it up before the concentration of Lawsone starts to decrease.

The suppliers were furious at our decision to discontinue the sales.

As we disposed of 20,000 bottles that were in stock, we were saddled with a debt of over 10 million yen. Although taking on the debt would temporarily make business difficult for us, we believed that it was important to not betray our clients' trust in our products. In the long run, I think we learned a lot from this failure. I can only say that now because I spent many sleepless nights leading up to this decision.

I was afraid that we would go bankrupt.

I quickly realized that it would be difficult to repay this debt with the profits from the hair salon alone. As a hair salon that only does cuts and henna, we probably saw the lowest spending per customer of any hair salons in the Minami-Aoyama area. We could only treat a fixed number of customers a day so the profit is limited. Should we sell our stocks and become publicly traded? There were times when I thought that I could hear the devil's whispers in my head. Still, I stuck with my original decision.

My sister, whom I had not seen for a long time, closed her own savings account and offered me some cash to help me finance my business. I guess she must have noticed my distress. I felt ashamed of myself for causing even my sister to worry, who had nothing to do with my plans.

Looking back on it now, this decision was not a mistake. If I had not made this decision, I would not be where I am today. However, it was a hard time, and I often felt as if I was being chased by something.

Henna is best delivered in powder form. We should not seek too much simplicity or convenience. Otherwise, it will draw negative consequences. If we try to minimize the amount of effort we put in, though, we are getting our priorities backwards.

This experience taught me that everything would be pointless if I did not offer what people would really need in the future exactly how they needed it rather than trying to meet the demands of today.

Henna containing chemicals widely distributed, resulting health hazards reported in the news — Japanese henna importers are to blame for their lack of knowledge in this matter

Around the year 2000, various companies began selling henna. In addition to hair salons, sales began at drugstores and major online shops, expanding the market.

Although we were happy to see the spread of henna, a problem arose after a while. Some products that were labeled as 100% plant-based were actually mixed with heavy metals and paraphenylenediamine, a chemical substance used as a hair dye. Originally, "black henna," which dyes hair black was available for low cost in India, and was imported. Japanese distributors and dealers were uninformed about henna, and many of them were told by their Indian business partners that it was 100% henna.

When looking around, we noticed that many people who used henna around the year 2000 thought that it darkened their hair too much. Not only black henna, but also artificial coloring is used to make the green color of the henna powder brighter, and this coloring contains little or no pigment Lawsone. Some henna products meant to be less dark used this kind of henna mixture and had picramic acid as well as sodium mixed with the henna powder so that it gave the product an orange tint unlike authentic henna. Although there have been many issues with chemical powders in henna, there is no need to worry about pesticides because henna grown on farms does not require them. However, chemicals may be added at the factory where the henna is harvested, dried and processed into powder. The level of sanitation in the processing plants was also questioned because improper regulation could lead to bacterial contamination.

The National Consumer Affairs Center (NCC) began to receive complaints of rashes, redness, swelling and other problems caused by the use of chemical-mixed henna. This was considered a serious problem, and in 2006 and 2007, the center published a special magazine titled, "Tashikana Me," to examine the use of henna. The feature article in the October 2006 issue reported that eight products of 12 manufacturers (total 14 products) did not contain the appropriate amount of Lawsone pigment. The article listed the problems with the verified henna products in the market and requested that the industry and government make improvements.

- Although some products were labeled as hair dye with henna, little or no henna pigment Lawsone was detected.
- The actual dye performance was low because many products

contained little or no pigment Lawsone.

- Although there were no dyes (such as paraphenylenediamine) used in permanent hair dyes in this survey, some products had no label indicating that a patch test was required in advance.

None of the products examined in 2006 used dyes (such as paraphenylenediamine) used in permanent hair dyes.

In the July 2007 issue of "Tashikana Me," the following requests were made to the industry:

- Unapproved henna products that contain oxidative dyes should not be sold for use on hair at all. They could be used for wigs instead.
- Improvement should be made to reduce misleading labels on products sold as being "for wigs" or "miscellaneous goods" so that consumers will not mistakenly use them on their hair.

We were surprised to find even more problematic henna on the market than in the previous year. This report actually had a negative impact on the distribution of henna. It was very difficult to find and import reliable products that were 100% henna.

When I started importing henna in 1995, I ordered samples and started dealing with the companies I thought were the best. After the products arrived in Japan, the content of the henna was analyzed and examined by an official institution. Although we only dealt with 100% henna products, we found one case with oxidized dyes or other chemicals after several inspections.

We were able to continue doing business with another company for a long time after that. However, when the company representative was replaced, the purchasing partners changed, and I felt that the quality of henna deteriorated, such as poor dyeing. When we looked into it, we found that the amount of Lawsone, the henna pigment component, was also lowered. I felt that it is very difficult to find good quality henna.

Although some of the henna imported into Japan today comes from North Africa and the Middle East, most still comes from India. Among the varieties that come from there, henna from Rajasthan in north-western India is said to be of the highest quality, and many products are imported to Japan from this region.

India's only government-controlled henna market is in Sojat in the state of Rajasthan, which is said to deal with the highest quality henna and stacks of plant henna collected from many farmers.

Henna is purchased from this market by specialized traders and transported to factories where it is processed into a powder. It is difficult for most processing companies to track down the details of where and how the henna comes from.

It was important to find a henna company that knew the traceability of its henna, from the farm to commercialization. If the data was also approved for its accuracy by a third-party certification organization, we figured it would be safer and more reliable for daily use.

Based on the number of complaints to the National Consumer Affairs Center in 2006 and 2007, as well as the article in "Tashikana Me," we felt that it was necessary to seek out safer and higher quality henna.

We decided to look for a company in India that handled henna certified by Ecocert. Established in France in 1991, Ecocert is one of the world's largest organic certification organizations, and I knew that I could trust them.

We find a company committed to pursuing "what is necessary for mankind" in India — CNP focuses on activities for a sustainable society

In 2009, when I was looking for a company in India that had obtained the Ecocert certification, I came across Cultivator Natural Products, or CNP. It grows not only henna but also many other kinds of medicinal plants organically, without pesticides, on their own farms. The company does not use chemicals, oxides, heavy metals, GMOs (genetically modified organisms), or other ingredients that may be harmful to health or the environment, nor does it conduct animal testing. CNP does not pollute water or soil in the manufacturing process, and it uses solar energy.

When I found CNP, I was very excited. I immediately contacted the company and ordered samples, and I was more than satisfied with the quality of their products.

After henna started being treated as cosmetics in Japan, instead of miscellaneous goods, our brand Lakshmi obtained a license to manufacture and sell cosmetics. I felt that with CNP we would be able to deliver high quality products with confidence, even though we were preparing to purchase directly and sell to the public without a wholesaler. This was also what I had been longing to achieve, and I felt like I could see a path of hope spreading before me.

CNP is based in Jodhpur, in the northwestern Indian state of Rajasthan.

The current chairman, Narayan Das Prajapati, succeeded Sonamukhi Udhyog, the previous owner of CNP, in 1999. At that time, the company was already certified by Ecocert. The following year it began selling its certified organic products domestically, and even overseas later on. In fact, the company's history goes back even further, to 1988, when Narayan was only 50 years old. Until he started CNP, Narayan had been in the textile business (textile business producing fabrics) and operated several factories. As someone who cannot create water or air, he thought he should not be polluting either of these resources, and decided to shift his work to bring out the best of plants, while respecting nature.

"I want to do business in a way that preserves nature and does not destroy it," he believed.

He said he wanted to work in such a way that he could give back to Mother Nature, and he did.

Narayan's business is focused on growing medicinal plants and using them for our daily lives while keeping the process sustainable.

In India, medicinal plants have always been highly demanded and recently their farming business has flourished. The fields for medicinal plants are very different from those that are used for other crops.

At one point, though, people in India prioritized farming grains, pulses, oil crops for oil extraction, sugarcane and cotton to earn higher income. In 1947, when India became independent from Britain, trees were considered a nuisance because they prevented food production. They were cut down. When farmers began using tractors, the trees were sold off as building materials for cash instead.

The trees, such as arm (mango), amla and kaitha (feronia elephantum) cut down, were carefully nurtured by the ancestors of present-day

Indian people and generated income for the farmers. If there is a tree, it produces fruit. But this process has ceased to exist due to logging.

Not only is this the case, but the biodiversity that the farmlands cultivated has been completely destroyed as well. We have forgotten how important trees were to the farmland. As a result of their failure to preserve the wisdom of their wise forefathers, the financial troubles of farmers became worse and worse. Trees are not harmful to crops, but rather beneficial instead. A blessing from the trees will help us escape from poverty.

"We must plant and grow new trees," Narayan says earnestly. "Biodiversity is important for medicinal plants, and we cannot grow medicinal plants or trees without it. Trees, vines and shrubs increase production and improve the quality of the product grown. The trees produce flowers, fruits, leaves, bark and roots, which are used as fertilizer for the farmland. This fertilizer helps trees and medicinal plants grow, keeps the soil moist for a long period of time, and protects the soil on the surface of the farm from direct sunlight and rain. This harmony must not be disrupted." This is a belief that has been carried on by the current president, Tarun.

In January 2014, I visited CNP for the first time after I'd been in business with them for five years. I heard about their project to produce a more advanced henna.

Its farms, scattered around the Jodhpur region of Rajasthan, covered a total area of 400 square meters, and the headquarters building also has a large farm adjacent to it. Each farm is neatly constructed with a drip irrigation system to prevent soil erosion.

Narayan Das Prajapati, chairman

Tarun Prajapati, managing director

“We try not to pollute the water or soil, and we use solar energy to produce, process and package our products,” representatives of the organization told me.

I felt that the medicinal herbs growing there were full of vitality. I fell in love with the farm because I could feel the beauty and strength of nature with my whole body there. I can also smell the pleasant scent of earth.

Bringing “authenticity” to both products and the world, aiming to alleviate poverty in the region

— The chairman of CNP, an expert in medicinal herb cultivation, conveys the cultivation method in detail

“I want to tell the truth.”

“I want to help the rural poor.”

When I had a conversation with him, Narayan's son, Tarun Prajapati, who is now the managingdirector of the company, looked straight at me and said, "I am always searching for what is necessary for mankind." These words resonated deeply with my heart.

I wanted to work with him.

From the first day I met Narayan and his son, I was strongly drawn to their way of life and approach to their work. I still feel attracted by their way of life and approach to their work.

CNP manages not only its own farms but also contract farms, which totaled about 8 million square meters in 2014. The company is able to harvest medicinal herbs using organic and pesticide-free methods at their best condition. High quality medicinal herbs harvested this way are processed for pharmaceutical, food, cosmetic and other uses and exported around the world.

One such example is the organic herbal tea sold by a brand called, "Pukka" in the U.K., which has recently become popular in Japan as well. The herbs grown by CNP are also used in this tea. During my visit to India, which coincided with a visit by the president of Pukka, I was able to discuss the company's corporate activities and its contribution to society with him.

CNP's distribution channels are certified for organic medicinal plants and now extend beyond the domestic Indian market. They supply to the international market as well. The size of the farm has also expanded to cover more than 3,000 acres (about 1,200 hectares) as of 2020. The medicinal plants harvested there are processed in a plant that's 100,000 square feet (about 9,290 square meters) in area. It produces about 80 kinds of herbs.

As stated before, Rajasthan is a home to the largest government-controlled henna market in India, which offers a place to sell plant henna harvested from farms to processing companies.

However, even though CNP is headquartered in western Rajasthan, it does not buy from this market. The company grows, harvests and transports medicinal herbs to its own factories, meaning that it manages and operates every manufacturing process from cultivation to processing and packing. Moreover, the company keeps records of where and how medicinal herbs are grown, when they are harvested and when they are delivered to the factory. The results of inspections at key locations are also recorded. The entire history of a medicinal herb sold by the company is traceable. The company is certified by Ecocert. Both the company's mission statement and approval by a third party help build assurance and trust when doing business with other partners.

CNP values its own farms and contract farms because it wants to grow high-quality medicinal herbs to pass the process on to future generations, "deliver the real thing" and alleviate poverty" among farmers and agricultural workers. At the root of this wish is the constantly changing thought, "What is necessary for mankind as a whole?"

Chairman Narayan has developed up to 50 cultivation methods for herbs and organic farming systems. A founding member of a government agency for medicinal herbs, he is also a member of India's national medicinal plant board, the Indian Ministry of Health and Family Welfare, and is considered a leading authority on the cultivation of medicinal herbs in India.

In 2003, Narayan published a 900-page encyclopedia of wild plants titled "A Handbook Of Medicinal Plants: A Complete Source Book," which is a compilation of 1,346 species of medicinal plants studied over 20 years, from the time he was 50 years old. This is the first book of its kind to be published in the world.

The book, which resulted from his long research on weeds and wild-flowers found all over the world, offers a comprehensive and practical guide for anyone interested in the agricultural cultivation of medicinal herbs. Narayan says that he wanted to share his knowledge and wisdom through this publication in order to train farmers in India.

In addition to the handbook, Narayan has appeared in a radio lecture series and on television in cooperation with government agencies on medicinal herbs and their cultivation. Through free leaflets and numerous training programs, he has guided more than 4,000 farmers on the path to medicinal herb cultivation.

His son Tarun is also an expert in herbal cultivation, post-harvest management, herbal remedies, arid zone ecology, rain-fed irrigation systems and organic farming. He is a medicinal botanist with a Master's degree in Herbal Medicine from the graduate school of the National University of Gujarat Ayurveda. He has presented many papers at international conferences and lectured at national and international seminars. He studied marketing in the United States and is widely considered an expert on agriculture and export.

Tarun joined CNP in 2005. Like his father Narayan, he has taken up the training of herbalist farmers and published the monthly "AMALTAS" magazine (which boasts a circulation of 50,000 copies a month), which is available at a discounted price. As editor-in-chief, he is dedicated to spreading knowledge about the cultivation, marketing and uses of medicinal herbs.

Most of the Rajasthan region of India where CNP is located is desert, which makes it difficult to obtain water. People have to walk many kilometers to get drinking water. Life is so difficult that children are often forced to work instead of going to school. Drugs are rampant in the impoverished communities, and the addiction rate rises steadily.

The crime rate is high, and many people are also dying of diseases due to poor sanitation. The hope to improve this difficult living situation for people so that they can lead a happy life is the motivation behind CNP's actions as a company.

CNP's priority is to ensure that its farm workers are paid fairly and that the purchase price of medicinal herbs paid to contract farms is also fair. The company has built houses on its farms and strives to ensure that the workers have a comfortable and hygienic living environment.

On contract farms, CNP also provides housing for farmers who need a home. On the most poverty-stricken contract farms in the northern part of India, CNP's associates are building restaurants and preparing food for the people of the community.

The company offers its workers sufficient salaries so that their children and the children of contract farm workers can attend school. By putting an end to the economic situation that forces people to work at the expense of their education, CNP encourages people to trust school education and attend school.

CNP grows the final medicinal herbs for its products on its own farms, which creates jobs for people in the community. By increasing the number of contract farms, it can purchase medicinal herbs from farmers at a fair price, so it does this as well. As a leading expert on herb cultivation methods, Narayan teaches farmers how to use them for free. This enables CNP to harvest high quality medicinal herbs with traceability. This is a positive corporate practice that benefits everyone.

Narayan says that medicinal herbs must be grown without pesticides and that the quality of plants in general changes depending on the amount of pesticides they contain. For example, henna grown without pesticides has a higher amount of the red pigment that was discussed in earlier chapters.

If medicinal herbs can be harvested in good condition without pesticides, this means that the final product is of high quality, which in turn means that CNP is able to deliver the product with high efficacy. In addition to efficacy, pesticide-free cultivation protects the health of the farmers and the land, resulting in a corporate practice benefiting both humans and nature. CNP's practice to alleviate poverty has not stopped since I came to know the company, and they have continued to offer various benefits. It has established a health care system that provides regular medical checkups for its employees, who are contract farmers, and their families as well.

As a contribution to the community, the company also provides support for orphans by distributing free sweaters to public school children in the winter. At the same time, it provides assistance to children battling illnesses.

CNP employs local unskilled workers at its factories and provides extensive programs that will train them to become highly skilled workers. Wages are also higher than the minimum wage required by India's Minimum Wage Law. In addition to these policies, the company ensures that workers have sufficient vacation time.

In 2019, CNP received the "Fair for Life" certification from Ecocert, which certifies fair trade products for workers, their families, and the community. This is the first time in the world that an organic henna product has been certified as Fair Trade.

"Fair for Life" is based on three fundamental principles: respect for human rights and fair working conditions; respect for the ecosystem and the promotion of biodiversity, sustainable agriculture practices; and respect for betterment of local impact. The first two principles are practiced by CNP as described previously.

As for the principle of improving and enhancing local impact, CNP offers support to orphans infected with HIV/AIDS. Providing food, clothing and shelter can only accommodate the needs of children temporarily. What's more important is what comes after that. The company is trying to create an environment where these orphans can one day enjoy working with a sense of accomplishment in the future. This is one way to support them so that they can be self-sufficient by paving their own future.

In particular, CNP considers supporting women's rights in the workplace to be an important issue and has established an entity just for this purpose. The effort is designed to create an environment where women can work with enthusiasm, without worry about mistreatment.

CNP has more than 500 business partners worldwide, many of whom export herbal raw materials. After export, they are then turned into finished products, such as organic herbal teas. CNP has established another entity for import and sales that imports the finished products from these partners and sells them in India. This company, which is currently developing a new business model, is planning to become a future workplace for orphans infected with AIDS as well.

CNP imports high quality products from its trusted business partners and spreads the word across India. I feel that this practice is a way of supporting the economy that is positive for everyone.

I have also been asked by the company if I would like to export and sell our brand Lakshmi's original products. I told them that I would like to help in any other aspect as much as possible, outside of exporting the products.

Clean rooms and state-of-the-art equipment — CNP has well-equipped research and testing labs

As a company that was started by an expert in medicinal herb cultivation, CNP is well equipped in techniques that preserve the active ingredients of medicinal herbs to the maximum extent possible.

In addition, experts in Ayurveda, the traditional medicine of India, have adopted cutting-edge technology to ensure that the herbs are grown, harvested, dried, processed and stored in an ideal environment for the plants. It is important as well as the quality control is consistent. The plant-growing process is commercialized in an ideal environment for such a process.

The company has established its own system for traceability, which records the history of when and where the products were grown, harvested, processed, packaged and inspected, as well as the inspection results.

When we actually asked them questions, they always responded right away. They could immediately tell me when and where the henna powder that I was looking at was harvested, or what state it was in after it was dried.

The processing factories are equipped with modern laboratories based on high European and American safety and hygiene standards. Since 2015, solar panels have been installed on all farms and factories, and the entire company operates on 100% green energy.

A tour of the factory reveals that the company has invested considerably in its equipment. It is clear that Tarun won't hesitate to invest in producing what's genuine. I am sometimes surprised by his bold moves as I watch him from the sidelines. He is making so much progress so fast even though he is young, still in his 30s.

In 2016, a new state-of-the-art plant was being built in a clean room comparable to a hospital operating room in accordance with the aforementioned European and US construction standards.

The cleanliness levels at the new plant were just like an operating room at a hospital.

At 8 p.m. on Nov. 8, Indian Prime Minister Narendra Damodardas Modi suddenly announced that high-value banknotes would be abolished at midnight on Nov. 9. The Indian government has been trying to prevent counterfeit and fraudulent currency storage. As a result of Modi's decision, the Indian government abolished the 1,000-rupee bill, the highest bill in circulation, and the next highest 500-rupee bill as well with an aim to eradicate counterfeit bills and illicit money gained through abuse of power. The new 2,000-rupee bill will be released in the next 10 days and the new 500-rupee bill in the next few weeks. The government requested that people deposit old bills and make their withdrawals in new bills. The government said that these exchanges, however, should be limited only to 4,000 rupees, and the withdrawal from the bank up to 20,000 rupees per week.

This brought chaos in Indian banks and delays in remittances.

CNP, which was building a new factory, had to stop making payments for construction work and precision machinery purchased from overseas companies due to this confusion. The company also had to worry about paying its employees. More than 90% of Indians pay in cash. It was difficult to suddenly offer digital payments to employees. Even if the company could do it, the employees who received the payment would be confused.

The construction was temporarily suspended, and CNP faced a crisis. But for Tarun, his youth and skill helped him easily overcome this hardship.

"If there is anything I can do, please let me know. If you need funds, I will do everything I can," I told him right away when I heard about the financial issues.

"Thank you. I will try to do what I can now," he replied.

Tarun sounded committed to find a solution and move forward in the face of the crisis. Many of his business partners in Europe and the United States offered to help him in any way possible. This meant that many of his business partners shared his business principles.

His desire to deliver "genuine products" and to give business profits back to the people who work for him. His commitment to "eliminate poverty" moves the hearts of his business partners. His clients are in various industries ranging from food and beauty to even the medical industry. Once you start doing business with CNP, you find it difficult to find any products of the same quality.

I did everything I could to support Tarun. I wanted to support him because I didn't want to lose his company and I strongly felt that it would be impossible to find another one that produces such a high quality product. I never expected to get paid back for the support I offered him. Later, though, I learned that he considered my support as an advance payment.

"I must return the favor," he often tells me. I truly trust his work.

Tarn is much younger than I am, but there is a lot for me to learn from him. I respect him.

The construction stopped for about three months. I think Tarun spent many days feeling anxious during this period of time. In March 2017, though, the new plant was successfully completed with a clean room equipped with the state-of-the-art technology.

Besides the factory section, it also has an inspection lab and a research lab with state-of-the-art equipment.

In addition to processing herbs for pharmaceuticals and foods, CNP has been producing and marketing its own original merchandise, mainly henna, shampoos and other cosmetics at the new factory since 2017. These products have also received Ecocert, USDA and Leaping Bunny certifications, which indicate that they are not tested on animals, and that they also comply with 2019 vegan certifications.

The company has a well-equipped design and printing room, which enables it to design and produce packaging in-house. Tarun studied at a graduate program of Ayurveda University, and he also devotes himself to the research of Ayurvedic medicine, so the company also has a well-developed medical facility.

The author (right) and Tarun in front of a solar panel system in the field near the factory

Sales of CNP's safe, high-quality henna — The evolution of beauty-related herbal products

Meeting CNP and the Prajapatis helped me learn what I had always wanted to do with henna and other medicinal herbs.

I started selling three CNP products in 2017; Organic Herb R, which is 100% henna; Organic Herb B and Organic Herb C.

Organic Herb B was made from four herbs; Indigofera tinctoria (indigo), henna, aloe vera and cassia auriculata leaf. A combination of Organic Herb B and R is used to change the orange-tinged hair color to a lighter color tone. Organic Herb C, made from 100% cassia auriculata leaves, was used as a treatment.

We were very pleased to be able to launch such a high quality herbal powder hair care product at Lakshmi.

In 2016, CNP dried and milled about 10 kinds of herbs to create 20 dyes for gray hair. It was considered difficult to mix various herbs while maintaining the active ingredients of each herb and to dye gray hair in various colors by using herbs. However, CNP's new technology has made this possible.

With the newly developed advanced milling technology, the amount of Lawsone pigment composition has increased even in the pure henna powder. The finer particles of powder also help reduce lumps when the henna powder is dissolved in water. When the particles were less fine, the powder was dissolved in water and had to be left for a day to increase the amount of Lawsone pigment composition and enhance its effect. Because the new product has a finer powder, it can be used immediately after dissolving in water to obtain a higher amount of pigment.

CNP began sales in Europe and the U.S. In 2017, a new plant was completed, and the manufacturing of their beauty products was moved there. I began planning what products I could sell under my Lakshmi brand when CNP launched new product lines.

Since 2014, I have visited CNP in India twice a year; fall and spring, and when Tarun comes to Japan, we meet at my hair salon.

After discussing new products that CNP launched in 2016 and determining which of those we planned to sell at Lakshmi, we finally chose a total of five products (including henna) and created our original packaging for them. I decided to design the packaging myself and we asked CNP to print it for us.

In 2018, Lakshmi launched its EcoVeda product line, which is called,

"Organic Herbal Hair Color."

What was new about this line of products? Everything was the same, especially the quality and the way the henna was grown and harvested, but the processing technology had evolved.

The milling technology became more advanced, and it is now possible to produce finer particles of powder without destroying the plant tissues in it. Adding nitrogen to the package after the powder is packed helps prevent oxidation. Sterilization prior to encapsulation has also become more rigorous.

We decided to follow what is said to be the world's most rigid regulation for the composition and safety of cosmetics set by the EU (specifically the regulation number EC 1223/2009). We also use fluidized air high-pressure steam sterilization, which is stricter than the Japanese standard. CNP chose to sterilize its hair care products, which are treated as cosmetics, in the same way as food. It is currently using the same method that is used to sterilize tea leaves in Japan.

When CNP began using this new technology, Tarun asked me, "What about the products you sell at Lakshmi, Mr. Morita? Do you want to keep the same sterilization techniques as before?"

Some bacteria are beneficial, so I was concerned about killing most of them in the sterilization process. I thought that the customers of the world need to experience a certain degree of symbiosis with bacteria, and bacteria might affect the colors of henna dye in a good way as well.

In the future, however, there is a possibility that bacteria will be controlled under much more strict guidelines in Japan, to the same standards in the EU and the U.S. We should not wait until their laws set the guidelines. Rather, we should act ahead and improve the quality of our cosmetics before the new standards go into effect. We have decided to comply with the European standards because we believe that it is important to improve the quality of cosmetics and to give consumers guaranteed safety.

After launching my new product at Lakshmi in 2018, there were still some things left to consider. I was concerned about the fact that many kinds of herbs were being mixed into the formula. There are customers with allergies to plants, just as some people have hay fever. If more plants are used, there will be a higher probability of allergic reactions. Some dermatologists have suggested that people today are more sensitive to allergens than in the past.

We wanted to make the color "orange" by using only henna and four other gray hair dyes, which would require mixing fewer kinds of herbs. I had been thinking of recipes for some time, and the medicinal effects and colors of herbs as well.

I wanted to make the new products as safe as possible so that many people would be able to use them. I told Tarun, who was in Japan in August 2018, about the recipe I had created. He agreed to make a prototype for me in India. I also told him that I wanted to make the 25-gram bag into a 100-gram bag, because I wanted to improve the packaging and reduce waste.

We then discussed powdered shampoo. Noticing the fragrance of roses in the powder, I also proposed that Lakshmi should make a face pack with rose fragrance. Tarun pointed to the benefits of amla charcoal. It removes dirt and odor from skin and has a strong adsorptive power, which makes it an effective deodorant as well. When used as a facial cleanser, it is said to remove excess material from the skin. Amla charcoal was already getting popular in Europe and the U.S., and I was eager to follow Tarun's suggestion.

Upon returning to India, Tarun informed me that he would show me a prototype when I visited him in March.

So I went to India in March 2018 and 2019 to test the user experience and tint of the hair color. In May 2019, I finally launched the new series of products, called, "2019 Organic Herbal Hair Color." The product is Lakshmi's original idea, and is sold only in Japan. The "Orange" is only made of henna, while the "Dark Brown," "Deep Chestnut," "Blond" and "Red" are made from a mixture of three kinds of herbs. The products launched in 2017 consisted of eight to nine kinds of herbs-a big reduction. I was pleased to produce the henna and hair color products that best satisfied this new time period.

Meeting the people at CNP gave me great hope. They listen to what I want to do and tell me what is possible. They then help me make the best possible products through solid research and testing.

We do not want to destroy beautiful hair in the name of cutting-edge fashion. Rather, we want to create a positive cycle that preserves the beauty of the hair by maintaining the natural beauty without doing anything unnecessary and to enhance the beauty the hair has. I would like to turn hair fashion into a positive cycle. We want to create a world where people can enjoy beautiful hair and skin even in old age, without hurting anyone who works in the beauty industry or receives treatment.

By relying on plants that grow in nature to make beauty products, instead of chemicals, we can avoid destroying the environment itself by flushing them down the drain after each use. This is important for creating a sustainable world.

Finding CNP has laid down a future where I can realize my various aspirations.

List of herbs used in Lakshmi's henna and hair color

Product name	Scientific name
2019 ORANGE	Lawsonia inermis
2019 DARK BROWN	Indigofera tinctoria
	Lawsonia inermis
	Cassia auriculata
2019 DEEP CHESTNUT	Indigofera tinctoria
	Lawsonia inermis
	Curcuma longa
2019 BLOND	Cassia auriculata
	Curcuma longa
	Matricaria chamomilla
2019 RED	Rubia cordifolia
	Beta vulgaris
	Ocimum sanctum

Chapter 3

Washing and conditioning the hair with new ideas and powdered herbs

High cleansing and moisturizing power puts a strain on the hair — Reviewing shampoo in use

After the hair coloring boom of the 1990s, numerous treatment products with strong moisturizing capacity were introduced to the market as consumers sought to make their dry, damaged hair look more beautiful. However, when the moisturizing effect is too strong, it causes various problems: It tends to get hair dirty easily and block pores. This, in turn, leads to the use of shampoos with stronger cleansing capacity. Stronger shampoos remove more sebum film, which dries out the scalp. When the scalp becomes too dry, the body senses that the scalp needs oil and begins to produce more oil, causing the skin to become greasy. Then the user begins to feel like shampooing every day.

This turns into a vicious cycle for the hair and skin. Without healthy skin, beautiful hair will not grow.

When people shampoo every day, a lot of shampoo products sell and the industry thrives. When hair becomes dry, the sales of treatment products increase. The shampoo industry does well, thanks to this cycle of caring for the unhealthy scalp and hair.

In recent years, more people in the medical and beauty industries have pointed out that the problem of hair care is that people wash their hair too often and that the strong shampoos damage the scalp and hair.

Sales and shipments of shampoo exceed 107.4 billion yen, according to the Ministry of Economy, Trade and Industry's reports. Looking at the sales and the size of shipment, we can easily estimate the serious damage that has been done to the environment. What if we tried to halve the amount of shampoo we use?

Vegetable-based synthetic shampoo and treatment for transitioning away from damaged hair. — When some moisturizing is required

For the regrowth period of damaged hair, I created a liquid shampoo and treatment. The shampoo contains natural herbal extracts. The main purpose of the product was to remove dirt and oxidized sebum from the hair.

Although it is a synthetic shampoo, I wanted to make it from plant-derived materials that are biodegradable. Because it is liquid, it allows bacteria to multiply easily. Most shampoos on the market use paraben, a synthetic preservative derived from petroleum. However, we were able to take advantage of the antibacterial properties of three plant species when they are mixed, and we acidified the liquid to suppress the growth of bacteria. Our company was successful in creating a liquid shampoo free of petroleum-derived parabens.

We began sales of this product, which is manufactured by a Japanese cosmetics company, in 2013. It is important as shampoo and treatment are necessary for damaged hair as it requires a certain amount of moisturizing effect.

Our relationship with this company has spanned over 20 years. Prior to that, we purchased hair-care products including shampoo that we thought were of good quality from a different company that taught us about hair examination (see pages 62~63). Unfortunately, this company was dissolved. Its sales representative was very knowledgeable and taught me a lot, and I put a lot of trust in him. When the company went bankrupt, I was very disappointed and I was at a loss. While talking with him, though, I noticed that I had a budding desire to make my own shampoo in the future through consultation with sales people and engineers at cosmetics manufacturing companies. I felt that this was the time for a decision, and I set my sights on making it a reality.

We wanted to create a shampoo made exclusively of herbs for people with healthy hair or for those whose damaged hair has been restored.

The product would be made only from plants combined with medicinal herbs that are known to be effective in cleaning and preventing gray hair, as well as a few other important problems. People would be able to dissolve the product in water just before use, so there would be no need to add preservatives, and the effects of the herbal ingredients would be long-lasting. I shared my ideas for the herb combination with Tarun who is an expert in medicinal herbs, and tried making prototypes with him and CNP's research team. In the end, we came up with two types of powdered shampoo called "2019 Organic Herbal Shampoo—Migushi-Sumashi 1 and 2."

In the future, the company plans to offer biodegradable packaging that microorganisms will decompose to the molecular level when it is buried in the ground. The packaging would eventually turn into carbon dioxide and water, which will be recycled back into the natural world.

Wash healthy hair with herb-based products to keep its beauty — Hair cleanser friendly to both humans and environment

As mentioned earlier, shampoos changed dramatically in the 1990s, because of the popularity of hair coloring among young people. The damage caused by hair coloring led to people wanting shampoos with a higher moisturizing effect.

Then came a series of shampoos released by a major cosmetics company. The company spent more on advertising than any other cosmetics company in history. The publicity was designed to entice consumers to buy its products. Its shampoos were well-received by those who tried them on damaged hair as it temporarily moisturized their hair, making it feel as if the cuticles had been restored. The shampoo also made damaged hair more beautiful.

But in reality, the higher the moisturizing effect is, the more likely it is that the scalp will be trapped in the negative cycle of forcing people to want to wash their hair. Repeated use of petroleum-based shampoos breaks down the skin barrier. Hair coloring and perms applied in this scalp condition would be subject to enhanced percutaneous absorption. Chemicals would be introduced to the body more easily, which leads to damage to the health of the hair and body.

We wanted to make products that are friendly to both people and the environment. We wanted to improve the health of the hair and scalp as well.

With this in mind, we created the 100% herbal powders "Migushi-Sumashi 1" and "Migushi-Sumashi 2." We believe that our encounter with and ongoing relationship with CNP made this possible. The "Migushi-Sumashi" product series uses the power of herbs to remove excess sebum and dirt from the hair. We wanted to create a product that would not only be gentle on the hair and body, but one that would also work to enhance the health of human beings as well.

We believe that the increasing trend of thinning hair among men at a younger age is partly due to shampoo products and the frequent hair washing. Continued use of strong detergents causes dry scalp. The body, then, reacts to the need for oil and produces more oil, which clogs pores. This negative cycle, leading to thinning hair, is seen in both women and men though, not only men.

As I began my research on henna, I also learned about other herbs. I told Tarun about the specific herbs and their ratios I wanted to use. In support of my idea, the expert herbalist supervised the development work in CNP's lab.

When wild animals wash their bodies, they rub their bodies in water, mineral-rich mud and plants. So we decided to include mud in the "Migushi-Sumashi." We chose a white clay called Multani Mitti, which is certified by Ecocert. Due to sanitation reasons, it is difficult to use mud in the cosmetics industry, but since it is Ecocert-approved for safety and organic quality, we decided to use it. However, it was very difficult to wash off. We tried several times, but our attempts did not work.

So we decided to remove the mud and use three herbs that have cleaning properties in "Migushi-Sumashi 1"; soapberry (Sapindus mukorossi), soap pod (acacia concinna), and ziziphus spina-christi leaves.

Acacia concinna fruit and soap pods are rich in bubbling ingredients, which are known as bacopa monnieri in Japan and are said to prevent memory loss. So I decided to include them in our product. I selected the herbs to make the shampoos, keeping in mind that they would be absorbed through skin.

This is how "Migushi-Sumashi 1" came to be made from dried fruits and leaves of seven kinds of plants, and "Migushi-Sumashi 2" from five kinds of plants. The "Migushi-Sumashi 2" is designed for men, and contains ginger for a refreshing sensation when washing.

The name, "Migushi-Sumashi," is derived from hair washing ("Goha Sumimashi") in stories such as "Utsuho Monogatari (Tales of Utsuho)" and others of Japan's Heian Era (8th to 12th century).

The product series is gentle on both people and the environment.

When I think about the many times daily that each of the 250,000 beauty salons in Japan pour chemical shampoos and treatments down the drain, I worry about the earth. If each salon used environmentally-friendly products, we could do a lot to protect the environment.

Herbs used in Lakshmi's herbal powder shampoos

Product name	Scientific name
Migushi-Sumashi 1	Ziziphus spina-christi
	Acacia concinna
	Sapindus mukorossi
	Bacopa monnieri
	Eclipta alba
	Ocimum sanctum
	Azadirachta indica
Migushi-Sumashi 2	Hedychium spicatum
	Acacia concinna
	Sapindus mukorossi
	Ziziphus spina-christi
	Emblica officinalis

Part III

To the Future: The Potential of Plants

Chapter 1

With the help of plants

Versatility of plants usage in *tenugui* hand towels and dyeing waistcoats
— Introduction of synthetic dyes in Japan in the 19th century Meiji Era

The power of plants is superb. People in the past were aware of the medicinal effects of plants used in the dyeing of *tenugui* hand towels and kimonos. In the Edo Era (17th to 19th century), small hand towels known as *tenugui* were dyed in patterns using indigo as the raw dyeing material. Indigo is a strong antioxidant and has excellent sterilizing effects. It is likely that people carried *tenugui* around with them to prevent the growth of bacteria after wiping sweat off their hands. The *tenugui* was also used as a hand towel in the washroom because of the belief that it also helped suppress the growth of germs and keep pests at bay.

Women's waistcoat underwear was Akane colored—a color best described in English as madder red. Historically, Akane has been used as the color for underwear because the dye helps with irregular menstruation, works against inflammation, stops bleeding, and warms the body.

By the time the 8th Shogun, Yoshimune, took over in the 18th century, a dyeing hall was established in his Fukiage Gyoen estate inside the Edo castle, where dyeing research was conducted.

Dyeing took place in Japan with colors extracted from plant roots and leaves has more than 5,000 years of history worldwide. According to the Wajinden (a Japanese historical document), people already practiced indigo dyeing and madder dyeing in the 3rd century. Since around 1929, such dyeing methods were called *Kusakizome*, or dyeing with vegetables. This term was named by writer and herb-dyeing researcher Yamazaki Akira to distinguish it from dyeing with synthetic dyes, and it was first used in 1932, when the trademark was registered. Synthetic dyeing began to spread in the early Meiji period when artificial dyes were imported from Europe to Japan.

It's been 90 years since synthetic dyeing first became common. It is interesting to note that people used to wear clothes dyed with plants before then. It may take some time before the effects of synthetic dyes start to show on our bodies.

Potential of herbal medicines that take effect by being absorbed through the scalp — Taking advantage of the high rate of transdermal absorption (absorption through scalp)

We can see that the health effects of hair coloring have become common knowledge because of the Japanese government's warning on its website.

Percutaneous absorption of chemical substances can cause physical problems, because the scalp has the highest absorption rate of any part of the body. I wondered then whether I could make use of this effect in a positive way.

What happens if we put herbal medicine on our scalp? Won't it have a positive effect? I read a paper in CNP's archives that stated that henna improved liver function. I mentioned this during one of my workshops. A number of participants later reported that their liver health data was getting better. I am not suggesting that people with bad liver should be treated with henna necessarily, though.

My hypothesis that the transdermal absorption would have a positive effect on the body was tested through "Migushi-Sumashi" products. The reasoning that we had for using brahmi in "Migushi-Sumashi 1" is that this herb is described in botanical encyclopedias as a potential remedy for memory loss.

I would like to pursue this experiment further.

Using the effects of herbs alone to regulate the body — Commercializing whole body treatments and facial cleansers

Lakshmi's "2019 Organic Herbal Treatment Rose" is a full-body treatment. The petals of organically grown damask roses are dried and ground into a powder. Just before use, the mixture is stirred with lukewarm water until it becomes a paste so that it does not drip and goes onto the skin effectively. After a few moments, the body should be rinsed well.

I became interested in using roses after reading the book, "Rose and Brain" (K & K Press, 2016), by neurosurgeon Dr. Keiichi Amano, who talks about the fragrance of roses and its potential to enhance cognitive function. I figured that if there is even a slight chance of avoiding a risk of dementia, we should make a rose-scented treatment.

We chose a variety of damask rose called Rosa Damascena, which is highly aromatic. It is said that Cleopatra VII of ancient Egypt loved this rose. It is now widely cultivated commercially for rose water and oil for perfumes, cosmetics, and bath salts. Well-known for its ability to tone the skin, the rose has a smell that is effective in relieving stress. Although we can't clearly say whether or not it actually helps people avoid developing dementia (besides improving skin conditioning), it has great potential for the future.

In his article on "amla," Narayan of CNP wrote in an article that the amount of vitamin C contained in amla is different when it is grown without or with pesticides.

The reason the rose used in this case contains a sufficient amount of active ingredients is because of the effect of pesticide-free cultivation. By grinding it into a fine powder, it can easily be dissolved in lukewarm water, making the ingredients able to be absorbed by the body. Because the powder is nitrogen-filled, oxidation does not occur, and the fragrance of the rose remains strong.

When we met with Tarun, he told us about the power of charcoal when it was mixed with amla and we decided to formally release the face wash "Organic Herbal Cleansing Amla." It removes dirt and odor from the skin.

It is well known that charcoal has strong absorption power and that it is effective as a deodorant. It also removes grime from the skin when used as a facial cleanser.

Charcoal is said to invigorate the brain, rejuvenate, soothe coughs, and relieve skin diseases and headaches. Amla is a tree unique to India, which has been used as a medicine to treat illnesses since ancient times. Amla holds an important place in Ayurvedic literature, and is used as an ingredient in many everyday ointments.

When made into charcoal and used as a facial cleanser, it helps revitalize the skin and remove grime. Charcoal has many positive effects. Men who are concerned about foot odor should give it a try. The fine powder is a good thing, but because it is too fine it does not dissolve easily in water. People have complained that the facial cleanser made of charcoal paints their washbasin black or that it hardly washes off the face due to the charcoal particles being ground too fine.

Of course, I intend to improve on these issues. I wanted to commercialize this product first, because I had an intuition that there would be high expectations for amla charcoal in the future.

Timing is everything. When you decide to do something, it is important to take a step forward. Don't wait for "the right timing." I believe it is important to take the step when you feel committed to it, though

Chapter 2
Learning more about transdermal absorption and seeking potential in this new concept

Verifying the effectiveness of herbs with the help of CNP — Developing products that are friendly to both humans and Earth

I am eager to collect data and produce clinical results of the health effects of herbs through transdermal absorption, but I would also like to look at the data on side effects. For that, I contemplated asking Dr. Manoshi Sharma of Jodhpur Ayurveda University of Rajasthan, with whom I have a connection, because Rajasthan is where CNP is located, and Dr. Sharma is a good friend of Tarun.

When I asked Dr. Sharma about it, he told me that he could make a request through a Japanese Ayurvedic research and academic organization known as the Ayurvedic Society of Japan. This organization is led by Dr. Inamura Hiroe, who has made a great contribution to the spread of Ayurveda in Japan.

There are seven medicinal herbs that I am currently looking to have research studies conducted on specifically regarding the effects of their transdermal absorption on our health. They are called Lawsonia inermis, Indigofera tinctoria, Rubia cordifolia Azadirachta, Bacopa monnieri, Rosa damascena, and Emblica officinalis. According to the International Nomenclature of Cosmetic Ingredients, they are known in Japan as henna, nanban-ai leaf, akane stem, azalea indica leaf, bacopa monnieri leaf, damask rose flower and anmarok fruit, in that order.

When the effectiveness of transdermal absorption is proven, the beauty industry will surely be eager to consider how to use it in beauty care and to commercialize it. Currently, chemical shampoos, colorants and treatments are mainstream, but this will likely change. I am certain that the mainstream chemical ingredients will be replaced with 100% plant ingredients. The beauty industry as a whole, which once only thought about "destroying hair for the sake of business," will then believe in "making hair beautiful for economic prosperity" and "mainstreaming products beneficial for our health and the planet."

It will take time to obtain clinical results not only on the effects on hair and skin, but also on the health effects after transdermal absorption. I would like to do what it takes for them to work as quickly as possible, and I am planning to donate part of proceeds from Lakshmi's product sales for the research.

We are also planning to build a facility around an Ayurvedic hospital in Jodhpur, Rajasthan, by 2029. We would like many Japanese to experience Ayurveda firsthand.

Seven plants expecting effectiveness

Scientific name
Lawsonia inermis
Indigofera tinctoria
Rubia cordifolia
Azadirachta indica
Bacopa monnieri
Rosa damascena
Emblica officinalis

Appendix

These are websites where you can find information about hair and hair care.

*NOTE: The information on the linked sites is available as of March 2021 and subject to change or deletion in the future.

Websites for learning about hair, cosmetics, etc.

- Japan Hair Color Industry Association
  https://www.jhcia.org

- Japan Permanent Wave Lotion Industry Association
  http://www.perm.or.jp

- Japan Cosmetic Industry Association
  https://www.jcia.org/user/

- Japan Hair Science Association
  https://www.jhsa.jp/

Skin Damage Caused by Hair Dyeing

Report on the investigation into the cause of accidents and others based on the Consumer Safety Act Article 23 (1)

Skin Damage by Hair Dye, Consumer Safety Investigative Commission, October 23, 2015

- When accessed, there are two PDF documents; an overview and the content, on the website.

  https://www.caa.go.jp/policies/council/csic/report/report008/

- Summary

  https://www.dermatol.or.jp/uploads/uploads/files/news/s20151028_kezomegaiy-ou.pdf

- Useful information for daily life
  (Government of Japan Public Relations Office website)

  https://www.gov-online.go.jp/useful/article/201905/2.html

References

『トリートメントヘアカラー ヘナ 若々しく美しい髪を保つために』
（塩田要著／ゆうエージェンシー／1998年）

『美髪再生』
（塩田鹿納命著／メタモル出版／2008年）

『新版 なっとく! のヘアカラー&ヘナ&美容室選び』
（森田要・山中登志子著／彩流社／2015年）

『アーユルヴェーダの驚きの果実　アムラの真実』
（ナラヤン・ダス・プラジャパティ、タルン・プラジャパティ著、森田要監修、イナムラ・ヒロエ・シャルマ、森山繁翻訳／彩流社／2020年）

『ネパール・インドの聖なる植物事典』
（トリローク・チャンドラ・マジュプリア著・西岡直樹訳／八坂書房／1996年）

『ディオスコリデスの薬物誌』
（小川鼎三ほか編・ディオスコリデス著・鷲谷いづみ訳／エンタプライズ／1983年）

『民族植物学—原理と応用』
（C.M. コットン著・木俣美樹男、石川裕子訳／八坂書房／2004年）

『ファラオの秘薬―古代エジプト植物誌』
（リズ・マニカ著・編集部訳／八坂書房／1994年）
『ハーブの写真図鑑』
（レスリー・ブレムネス著・高橋良孝日本語版監修／日本ヴォーグ社／1995年）
『外因性内分泌攪乱物質「奪われし未来」をどう読み解くか!』
（平田雅彦著／研究資料〈非売品〉）
『経皮毒ハンドブック』
（稲津教久著／PHP研究所／2009年）
『毛髪の科学と診断』
（八木原陽一著／薬事日報社／2012年）
『発毛・育毛の新常識』
（東田雪子著／日刊工業新聞社／2003年）
『髪の大辞典 傷んだ髪は復元できる』
（社団法人日本毛髪構造機構研究会／徳間書店／2020年）
『サロンワーク発想だからわかる! きほんの毛髪科学』
（ルベル／タカラベルモント株式会社／株式会社女性モード社／2014年）
『天然染料の科学』
（青木正明著／日刊工業新聞社／2019年）
『髪の文化史』
（荒俣宏著／潮出版社／2000年）
『黒髪と美の歴史』
（平松隆円／KADOKAWA／2019年）
『人の暮らしを変えた植物の化学戦略』
（黒柳正典著／築地書館／2020年）
『生薬とからだをつなぐ』
（鈴木達彦著／医道の日本社／2018年）
『ボケたくなければバラの香りをかぎなさい』
（天野惠市／ワニブックス／2018年）
『薔薇と脳』
（あまのけいいち著／K&Kプレス／2016年）
『正倉院宝物（とんぼの本）』
（杉本一樹著／新潮社／2016年）

Afterward

The impact of COVID-19 shook the world in 2020.

Humanity stands at a major crossroads as we enter a new era.

Tarun Prajapati of India, president of CNP, and a good friend of mine, was quick to work on development of anti-coronavirus tablets with the advice of Dr. Manoj Sharma, Professor of Herbal Medicine at Jodhpur Ayurveda University and began distributing 10 million tablets free of charge to public institutions such as hospitals and the police department.

Tarun continues his research on Indian traditional medicine Ayurveda-based medicinal herbs and has combined traditional wisdom with cutting-edge technology to people around the world while still working to help the impoverished farmers.

Meanwhile, I am conducting research on the health effects of medicinal herbs through hair care and transdermal absorption.

I am certain that this new approach to beauty where we can take care of our health, hair and scalp with the help of medicinal herbs while enjoying their fragrance and texture will lead to a major change in the conventional wisdom and concept of beauty itself.

This book was also written to objectively understand the health effects of conventional beauty products, to better analyze them, and to change them for the better.

From the distant past up to now, human beings have benefited from the power of plants in various ways, such as using them for dyeing clothes and taking them as medicines.

These methods were born out of our ancestors' wisdom in regulating the energies of body and mind. Nowadays, we seem to be gradually forgetting about what is not visible, and our ancestors' wisdom is often interpreted as being superstitious.

These days, in the name of convenience and simplicity, many chemically synthesized products are developed. Companies that make them have seeking profit in mind rather than considering the health effects of chemicals on our body. This new trend has put a serious strain on the environment and is a grave concern for many.

We believe that product development should be based on the concept of "what is necessary for mankind."

It seems to me that there is no need to panic as long as we have a diet and environment that enhances our immunity. This has been proven with COVID-19, because the best preventative measures are having a good diet and a clean environment.

There are also concerns about the harmful environmental effects of hormones, not to mention the hair coloring and perms that are commonplace in beauty salons. The effects on the human body caused by percutaneous absorption are immeasurable. The amount of contaminated water discharged daily from more than 250,000 beauty salons in Japan is beyond imagination.

People around the world are now beginning to work toward a "sustainable" society that does not destroy the earth or exhaust resources. We must create a society together on and for a forever beautiful planet where people can continue to live in peace and abundance.

I believe that we should make an effort for the earth by looking at the beauty industry as one big contributor to nature preservation and as an environmentally conscious member of our future.

I wish for everyone to regain the beauty of their hair.

Through thinking about hair, we have learned and experienced many things and created new visions.

The only way to have beautiful hair is to retain our awareness.

April 8, 2021
Kamidoko
Kaname MORITA

The conditions necessary
to create the most beautiful hair
are that it be untouched by man,
and unguided by human thought.
It's perfect this way.
No animal can change the color or shape of its body.
No giraffe can become a zebra,
no lion can become a tiger.
So why do we change
what is given to us as "God's design"?
The only true shortcut
in beauty is to improve yourself.
In the past, the most important thing
was to support the economy
by making more products.

Our hair became damaged,
broken because we got caught up in this cycle.
From now on, I want to make sure
that the highest priority is "beautiful hair."
I hope you will listen to my proposal
and let more people know about the truth.
If we don't do anything,
the energy of our hair will keep being depleted.
Now is the time for us to switch to a new vision
and gain more beautiful,
more comfortable hairstyles
better suited to daily life.

Profile

Kaname MORITA

Born in Yamanashi Prefecture, Japan, 1958. Beauty Consultant. Owner of the Kamidoko hair salon and the cosmetics sales company Lakshmi Co. After graduating from Tokyo Max Beauty College in 1978, he opened his own beauty salon in Minami-Aoyama in 1984. Since 2009, he has held workshops throughout Japan on the concepts of "hair restoration" and "real beauty" and has published multiple books on the subject: "Henna Hair Color Treatments: To Keep Your Hair Young and Beautiful" (Kaname Shiota, Yu Agency, 2000 [previous edition, Yu Agency, 1998])『トリートメントヘアカラー ヘナ 若々しく美しい髪を保つために』(塩田鹿納命著、ゆうエージェンシー、2000年、旧版1998年) and "Beautiful Hair Regrowth: Let's Start Henna for Your Hair" (Kaname Shiota, Metamor, 2008)『美髪再生 髪にやさしいヘンナをはじめましょう』(塩田鹿納命著、メタモル出版、2008年). "New Edition: Nattoku! How to Choose Hair Color & Henna & Beauty Salon" (Kaname Morita and Toshiko Yamanaka, Sairyusha, 2015 [previous edition, Sairyusha, 2013])『新版 なっとく!のヘアカラー&ヘナ&美容室選び』(森田要・山中登志子著、彩流社、2015年、旧版2013年), "In Search of the Best Henna: The Miracle of Plant That Makes Hair Beautiful" (Kaname Morita, Tsubanasha, 2017)『最高のヘナを求めて 髪を美しくする奇跡の植物』(森田要著、茅花舎、2017年). He has also supervised works including "The Truth of Amla, the Amazing Fruit of Ayurveda" (Narayan Das Prajapati and Tarun Prajapati, editorial supervision by Kaname Morita, translated by Inamura Hiroe Sharma and Shigeru Moriyama, Sairyusha, 2020)『アーユルヴェーダの驚きの果実 アムラの真実』(タルン・プラジャパティほか著、森田要監修、森山繁翻訳).

Hair

In Search of Natural Beauty

2023年2月15日　初版第一刷

著　者　森田要 ©2023
翻訳者　松元ちえ、松元リップ覚
発行者　河野和憲
発行所　株式会社 彩流社
〒101-0051 東京都千代田区神田神保町3-10 大行ビル6階
電話 03-3234-5931　FAX 03-3234-5932
http://www.sairyusha.co.jp/

イラスト　おぐらきょうこ
装　丁　福田真一［DEN GRAPHICS］
印　刷　明和印刷株式会社
製　本　株式会社村上製本所

Printed in Japan　ISBN978-4-7791-2881-3 C00777
定価はカバーに表示してあります。乱丁・落丁本はお取り替えいたします。